# TRUE EMPATHY

## Melissa Forgey

BALBOA.
PRESS
A DIVISION OF HAY HOUSE

Balboa Press books may be ordered through booksellers or by contacting:

Balboa Press
A Division of Hay House
1663 Liberty Drive
Bloomington, IN 47403
www.balboapress.com
1 (877) 407-4847

Because of the dynamic nature of the Internet, any web addresses or
links contained in this book may have changed since publication and
may no longer be valid. The views expressed in this work are solely those
of the author and do not necessarily reflect the views of the publisher,
and the publisher hereby disclaims any responsibility for them.

The author of this book does not dispense medical advice or prescribe the use
of any technique as a form of treatment for physical, emotional, or medical
problems without the advice of a physician, either directly or indirectly. The
intent of the author is only to offer information of a general nature to help
you in your quest for emotional and spiritual well-being. In the event you use
any of the information in this book for yourself, which is your constitutional
right, the author and the publisher assume no responsibility for your actions.

Any people depicted in stock imagery provided by Thinkstock are
models, and such images are being used for illustrative purposes only.
Certain stock imagery © Thinkstock.

Print information available on the last page.

ISBN: 978-1-5043-2680-3 (sc)
ISBN: 978-1-5043-2682-7 (hc)
ISBN: 978-1-5043-2681-0 (e)

Library of Congress Control Number: 2015900750

Balboa Press rev. date: 03/24/2015

# Contents

# Preface

Years ago I walked into a nursing home as young adult. I cared for many wonderful people who had lost just about everything. Their lives had dwindled down to just a few belongings and some family. Sadly, some had nothing remaining with the exception of their own life. These are the most vulnerable people. Even as a young adult, I realized that we were letting them down.

I worked as a nurse's aide in nursing homes, a residential assistant in assisted living facilities, and a home care provider. Eventually I owned and operated a home health business for about fifteen years. My experience as a business owner and employer offered me a different perspective on health care than I had had as a care provider.

Originally I thought I would share my experiences working in health care and the insights that I have gained through the years. I am frustrated that our elderly and vulnerable people still suffer despite advancements made in the medical field. As I continued to write this story, I realized that this is not so much a health-care dilemma but a human dilemma. This story shifted into a sharing on a very personal level. I hope this book will open the door to many conversations about how we can better help the elderly and vulnerable. I adamantly feel that we need to stop shutting the door on them. So now, for them, I share my story.

# Acknowledgments

I am grateful to have so many friends who have listened to me talk about writing this book for so many years. I am grateful for their encouragement. I am also grateful for their disbelief that I would ever get this project done.

I would like to thank my friends who helped me type this book periodically throughout the years. Through this writing journey the computer has become an often-frustrating but less-frightening tool for me. I would also like to thank the people who offered me guidance and constructive criticism. Despite my resistance and stubbornness, your input has been valuable.

I would also like to thank my parents, who knew before their deaths that they would be a part of this book and offered their own guidance and insights, both knowing that they would not see the finished work. Thank you for your support.

# Introduction

True empathy hurts. This is how I refer to the feeling I have when I want to help someone so much that I can almost feel their pain. It is my desire to reach out to a stranger, or even to a stray cat or dog. It is the sense that their vulnerability is in some way connected to me and I must attempt to help. It is a feeling that will not leave me alone. True empathy is the driving force which motivated me to write this book and to tell my story, the story of those I have cared for and the story of my family.

# PART 1

# A Wealth of Humanity

# CHAPTER 1

# A New Journey

Who was this woman who was placed beside the receptionist's window like a decoration, and a haunting one at that? As I asked for an application, I avoided looking at her directly. This woman's face was defined by the outline of her skull. Her mouth gaped open, and sharp, piercing eyes peered through sunken holes. These eyes seemed to see into my subconscious; they made me feel uncomfortable. She was tied to a chair with a vest that had straps. Perhaps the vest was a weak attempt to cover the harshness of the restraint. She was wearing a plaid dress of multiple colors. Beneath her chair sat a muted-yellow puddle of urine. White bobby socks hung loosely on her spindly legs, contrasted by worn black loafers. I wondered, *Why did they tie her?* It was clear to me, even in my youth, that she could not walk. Perhaps the restraints provided some kind of false security for the nursing staff or the office staff, who were running to and fro, hardly noticing her.

*Are they all like this?* I asked myself as I handed my application to the receptionist.

"Call soon," she said. "We may have work for you."

I felt a lump in my stomach as I attempted to appear enthusiastic, all the time avoiding those piercing eyes from the woman tied to the chair by the receptionist's window. This woman, who seemed to be doing nothing, was stirring something deep inside me. I wanted to run away. I left the building, but the image of the woman stayed with me.

"Come on Tuesday," the nursing director told me when I called the next day. "You will need a uniform and white nursing shoes."

I was hired as a nurse's aide. I did not even want to be a nurse's aide, much less work in that environment. Yet I knew I did not want to return home to Ohio. Fear like a dense, dark cloud hung in the wings of my consciousness, creating chaos in any peaceful moment. *How did I get here?* I wondered.

Only a few weeks prior, I was sitting in a motel room with my mom and my brother, Matthew. The room smelled damp and musty. Matthew and I sat on one of the twin beds while Mom sat on the other, writing me a check. Mom slowly and carefully tore the check from the checkbook. She looked good for a woman who had just finished a long drive from Ohio to Vermont. Mom always looked nice. She wore a gray blazer, white blouse, and black dress pants. She possessed a natural sense of how to present herself—always just the right amount of jewelry and makeup applied so subtly that it looked natural. Her features were soft, and her smile was welcoming. Not today though—her face was set with no hint of warmth.

"This is it," she said as she handed me the check. "You will have to find a job or come home."

I said, "Thanks." As I studied the check for fifty dollars, I thought, *Hell of a graduation present.*

"Your dad and I have your graduation present at home. We will give it to you there," Mom said as if she had read my mind.

Matthew slid me his card. Inside was a check for two hundred dollars. I was surprised. He looked at me intently. He did not have to say anything. I knew if he had felt comfortable enough to do so, he would have said, "Here's some more time, Meliss."

Matthew looked very vulnerable. He had recently been discharged from the navy with a diagnosis of paranoid schizophrenia. His curly, brown hair was a little on the long side, and his thin, six-foot-three-inch frame shook, as the medications gave him tremors. Dad was noticeably absent. It was the night before my college graduation, and I wanted to party with my friends; yet I felt torn leaving Mom and Matthew in the motel room. My decision was to party with my friends. Part of me was relieved that Dad was not there. He said it was too hard for him to drive from Ohio to Vermont. I did not completely buy his story and allowed myself to feel hurt—a little. Anyway, this made spending time with my friends easier. Tonight I would party. Tomorrow I would go through the motions. And then I had to find a job. Life was loud then and cluttered with insecurities. Any quiet whispers that offered me solace fell silent, or perhaps I would not still myself enough to listen.

Procrastination was the result of my insecurities. Friends were familiar and safe. Employers were foreign and scary. I had completed my credit requirement a semester early. My parents had allowed me to stay in Vermont until graduation time, so I had hung out with my friends and occasionally looked for work. I had rented an apartment with a friend and an acquaintance I did not know very well. It made for cheap rent.

Now it was down to the wire, and my future was on the line. I felt if I returned to live with my parents, I would stagnate and never have a life. Lack of self-confidence was the biggest thing holding me back. After all, who would want to hire an awkward girl with thick glasses which didn't even fix her vision, who could not drive, who had a degree in fine arts, and who wore her insecurities on her sleeve?

Inaction was my tool of choice at the time. The division for the blind and visually impaired that assisted me in college also assisted me in my job search. My caseworker had suggested nursing homes, but I promptly dismissed the idea at the time. This idea I finally revisited, as other job options had not come to fruition.

My caseworker, whom I remember as a kind woman, drove me from nursing home to nursing home in an attempt to help me find a job I did not want. I developed a strategy of avoidance as I entered these facilities. Sometimes bad vision had its benefits, particularly when I did not want to see the environment for which I was applying for work. However, my plan fell short when I entered the last facility. There, right beside the receptionist's window, sat the gaunt woman with those piercing eyes.

I had mixed feelings as I called my family in Ohio to tell them I had a job. Matthew answered the phone. Upon hearing the news, he excitedly relayed the information to my parents. His enthusiasm for my success pleased me. He was a year and five days younger than I was. We were close as children. Our teenage years weren't so great, but now I knew he was in my corner. I always felt protective of Matthew. He wore his feelings on his sleeve, and that often created conflict in his life. Whenever I called Ohio, I spoke with both parents. One parent would be on the phone in the kitchen and the other on the phone in the master bedroom upstairs.

"I'm here," said Mom from the phone upstairs. Matthew handed the kitchen phone to Dad. Matthew's excitement was pervasive. I could tell that he was having a lucid day. I had learned to distinguish the Matthew I grew up with from his paranoid counterpart. Even in the midst of his disease, I had learned to recognize moments when I was speaking with him and not his illness.

On the phone, Dad usually dominated the conversations, and Mom occasionally chimed in. Dad even sounded a little excited as he said, "Hello." Still holding on to the predominant mood, I enthusiastically told them I was hired as a nurse's aide at a nursing home.

Dead silence.

About then I emotionally shut down on the conversation. *No support there,* I thought. I was on my own for this journey.

Many years later, Dad told me that I constantly dashed any mental images he had of me as an adult. On my first visit home after my first semester in college, Dad told me that he had imagined a much more sophisticated, well-dressed, well-spoken woman arriving at the airport. "I almost could see you carrying a small, white poodle," he said, half-smiling at the ridiculousness of his nonreality. Instead, I deplaned wearing work boots, jeans that had become too tight, and an overstretched patchwork sweater.

After my parents brought me home, I went upstairs to talk to Matthew, who had already gone to bed, as it was a late flight. I walked into his bedroom. He looked at me and said in his typical brutally honest way, "Boy, have you gotten fat."

With slumped shoulders, I slinked off to my bedroom. Matthew was blunt, but it was true and I could not blame the dorm dryers anymore.

My parents' disappointment in my new job only compounded my fears.

Tuesday arrived, and I entered the facility as I transformed my dread into numb acceptance. In every direction a harsh awakening to the human condition slammed my senses. I tentatively approached the nurses' station and introduced myself as the new nurse's aide. A nurse brought me to the adjacent wing and introduced me to Thelma, the nurse's aide who would be training me. Now I stood on the dock of new experience, and it was time to dive in. I took a deep breath, and off I went into unknown waters.

Mattie had an artificial leg. At first I thought it was a joke, but she really did have an artificial leg, and I had to help her remove it. Agnes dragged her walker behind her. She was all bent over, and at dinnertime she took out her false teeth and licked them clean. Helen moved at a snail's pace, and her slow movements made me want to laugh, but I didn't. Fred was all curled up in a fetal position. He had sores on every joint and on the back of his head. Some of the sores were open, while some had healed. He stayed in bed all of the time, as his body was too stiff and distorted to sit upright. Geraldine and Bernadette were in similar states of disrepair. Gertrude was a little lady who constantly talked about going to heaven. Pauline thought her husband hid in the cracks of doorways, and she walked around calling his name as she pressed her nose tightly to each door she found. Elaine was the safe haven. While disease prevented her body from moving, her welcoming personality and sense of humor drew the care providers to her for pleasant conversation and some sanity amongst the chaos.

Thelma, a tough-looking woman whose softness came through when she cared for these people, showed me the ropes. Never had I seen so much nakedness. Never had I seen bodies so riddled with disease or distorted with age. Never had I witnessed so many confused people, and never had I smelled or touched so much human excrement. We were not required to wear latex gloves then, and no matter how often I washed my hands, I could not completely remove the smell. Just before the shift ended, Marylou, who sat in a geri chair near the nurse's desk, vomited all over her tray and had diarrhea in her yellow pantsuit. Thelma and I took her into her room, lifted her onto the bed, and removed her clothes as best we could without getting feces and vomit everywhere. We bathed her and then washed her tray on the geri chair and rinsed the diarrhea from her yellow pantsuit. After throwing the last rinsed towel into the hamper, Thelma wiped her sweaty brow with her forearm. "Well Melissa," she said, "if you made it through today, you'll be just fine."

So there I was, at the end of my first day working as a nurse's aide. My crisp new uniform was stained with all sorts of organic material, and my nice, new, white shoes were now not so white. I felt tired but not exhausted. Something inside me had awakened. I now knew that deep within the cinderblock walls of this facility, with rooms painted in pretty colors as if to soften a sad reality, lay a wealth of humanity. These people were too vulnerable, too sick, and too lost in their lifetimes to be anyone other than who they were at that moment. All pretenses were lost. All that existed was the rawness of the human condition at its most fragile point. All I knew at that time was I did not want to leave. It is fair to say that my life changed that day.

# CHAPTER 2

# Unexpected Connections

Who were these people I bathed, fed, dressed, and cared for daily? Was it simply age, was it disease, or did they just give up? Every day the hallways of the nursing home became alive with brokenness. Yet it seemed to me, even in my youth, that no one really wanted to acknowledge that brokenness. That is, no one except for me. I tried to talk about it with my coworkers, only to be dismissed with trivial answers. I felt out of place. Perhaps they thought something was wrong with me. So I quieted myself for fear of losing my job.

Paralyzing fear—it held me back on so many things. I was so afraid of returning home. Home did not make sense at that time. Dad was sometimes crazy and controlling,

Matthew was difficult and draining to be around, and Mom was overwhelmed with it all. It was not warm and welcoming. I felt I had no power there, and I wanted my own life. Having no income meant going home to me then. So I coped with the pain I witnessed on a daily basis at the nursing home by developing a brutally crude sense of humor. Shock value was a familiar tool for me. In high school I would draw violent, gory pictures and revel at the reactions I received from people who looked at them. At the nursing home, I reveled at the look of disgust on my peer's face or the occasional challenge from someone trying to top my grossness. Alcohol was also an almost nightly escape. Deep down I did not like who I was in those moments. Life was uncomfortable, and I was running from that feeling as fast as I could. The only thing about running is at some point you have to stop to catch your breath—and then life catches up again.

I am sure some of the people I cared for caught glimpses of my youthful struggles to cope. Could they see my tearstained face or sense my inner pain? Yet these people accepted me, even liked me, and many told me they appreciated my care. So many people riddled with disease, be it disease of the body or of the mind, their condition had condemned them to a life of dependency. For many it became a life of aloneness while they waited for help. Somehow these people all managed to give me something. It was deeper than a thank you or a smile. Even those unable to respond affected me. The more I cared for these people, the more I realized that they were no different from me. It wasn't the job I valued as much as the people who needed my care. They all had a past and a prime of life. Some had been financially successful, while others were chronically poor. Some were pleasant and others unpleasant. Some were grateful and kind, while others seemed nasty and hateful. Each person coped differently with the loss of who they knew themselves to be, all the while living in an environment which they would not have chosen. Many had families. Some had none left. Others had pushed everyone away. I don't know how I would cope in such conditions.

While assisting Elaine as she ate her half a sandwich for supper, she explained to me that she only ate half so she would not become too heavy for us to lift. I thought about what a wonderful gift this woman was giving us. This woman who has lost everything, except for the movement of her arms, which was fairly limited and deteriorating steadily, was giving something to us. It is one of the best gifts I have ever received.

I remember Marge returning to the nursing home after attending her son's funeral. She was a stout little woman with a friendly face. Sometimes she could be very confused, but not this day. She was dressed all in black: black hat, black dress, black stockings, and black shoes. She slowly walked as if there was a great weight on her soul. She went into her room and sat on the bed. I followed and sat on the bed beside her. I put my arm around her. She leaned in a little. I felt the gravity of her sadness. We just sat.

"I should have gone first," Marge said quietly. "Even at my age, this is so hard." A single tear rolled from the corner of her eye and softly meandered down one of the deep lines of life in her face, until it fell off her chin onto her black dress.

I pulled invisible curtains, talked to people who were not there, all in an effort to make the confused person feel safe. As for the people who could do nothing, I learned to touch softly and move slowly, as not to create pain by pulling a taunt muscle or touching an open sore. One evening, while I was bathing a woman in this condition, I started to joke around with my coworker who was helping me. The woman we were bathing shot me a look and said firmly, "It's not funny!" It shocked me that she could even speak. Yet, what she said was true. For the moment I had forgotten she was a person. She was present and wanted to be focused on. It wasn't the joking that was the problem—it was the fact that we did not include her in our conversation.

How would I feel in their place? How much did their choices through their life's journey contribute to their condition presently? So many pasts, so many personalities, and so much unacknowledged pain—and I knew that I could not fix these people. However, I could make them comfortable for the night, and their gratitude for that simple act overwhelmed me.

As for the lady by the receptionist window, her name was Margaret. Every day her husband would come at mealtime and lovingly feed her. I could see her piercing eyes soften when she saw him walking down the hallway. I was no longer afraid of these people. I wanted to help them so much it hurt, and thus a true empathy was awakened in me.

CHAPTER 3

# People Who Suffer

Even then, in the early 1980s, I felt the care was archaic. Large roles of white plastic which we cut into various sizes provided the foundation for incontinent care. We would place the plastic on the chairs and on the beds. We would then cover it with draw sheets, regular sheets, or hospital blankets. On occasion we would find a quilted incontinent pad. There was no real system. We used what we could find. When the plastics got old, they cracked, and then the entire bed would get soaked with urine. I was tired of finding people on crinkled plastics, with the sheets half off and puddles of urine surrounding them. Often urine was cold and the people had deep creases in their skin from waiting too long to be changed. Did we value these people?

Then there was the force-feeding. We would stir blended food with milk or water and then pull the lumpy mixture into a large syringe and inject the substance into people's mouths. If anyone fought us while feeding, we were instructed to restrain their arms. Often the food was spit back at us. I hated mealtime. It wore on my psyche and tore at my consciousness. Beyond this, I was frustrated that no one wanted to acknowledge that there was something wrong with this picture.

During this time, Matthew had moved out for our parent's home and was renting a furnished apartment off campus. He was studying to become a naturalist. He would sometimes call me around two in the morning. We would talk for hours. Most of the time I talked to his illness, but there was always those few moments during our conversation when I knew I was speaking with my brother. He was lonely, a mentally ill man trying to interpret the world through distorted thoughts. His thoughts he had no control over most of the time. I learned to reason with those thoughts of his, and sometimes I was able to speak to the real Matthew. He wanted companionship, but he pushed it away. He had no more support from home than I did and that brought us closer, despite the unpredictable landscape of hallucinations and paranoia thoughts.

I began to think that being a nurse's aide was not a secure enough job. I resolved to go to nursing school. To my surprise the nursing program accepted me despite my visual impairment. At a time when I thought my parents might be proud of my acceptance into the nursing program, my father instead chose to disown me because I did not consult him on this decision. However, he did not disconnect; he would call me and let the phone ring one time and then hang up. He would repeat this every hour for several hours. He would also send postcards with written messages which only contained hurtful words. So my connection with my family became talking to Matthew through his mental illness and calling mom when she was at work.

My body ached. Nurse's aide work was draining, both mentally and physically. Nursing school was difficult at best, and I struggled to maintain a social life. The insanity and instability of my family also drained me. Life was truly cluttered, and I was losing myself in its chaos. I was so determined to become a nurse despite my vision. During the clinical at the hospital, we were instructed to study our assigned patient's charts at the nurse's station. When I looked up, there were about five nurses leaning on the counter staring at me. I knew what they were thinking, as my nose was probably touching the chart as I read it. Still, that did not discourage me. What did discourage me was a blood pressure wall monitor in the intensive care unit. I could not read the monitor on the wall. These were pre-digital times. The man whom I was caring for was vulnerable, and I knew I was not safe. So I left school with only a little more than a semester left until completion. I thought this might heal things with Dad, but it did not. So I chose to put myself into therapy.

It was the morning of June 27, 1984, when I next spoke to my parents together.

"Melissa?" Dad said. "This is your dad and mom. Your brother is dead." Matthew had put a bullet into his head. I did not know how to digest this. I had seen death at the nursing home. For this death, however, I was not prepared.

## CHAPTER 4

# Journeys Will End

"Look at me. Listen to me. Value me," Matthew could have said. "See my pain. Feel my loneliness. I suffer with thoughts that frighten me. Why does everyone look away?"

The people I cared for in the nursing home could have said, "See my body; it is not as it used to be. Listen to me, though my words may be muddled and my thoughts unclear. I am here now as I am. Please value me."

It was all the same: people suffering from various diseases that caused them to be different, being tucked away. Yes, some people cared, but not enough. People who are being ignored can give up on themselves. Some fade into the corners, some become loud, and others get lost in their own confusion. Be it conscious or unconscious neglect, it is still life-threatening. Perhaps our neglect of these people is the true disease.

A few weeks before Matthew committed suicide, he called me. He wanted me to join him in disconnecting from our parents. Even though our family was in the thralls of dysfunction, I could not make that commitment to him. He also asked me if he could come to Vermont and stay with me. I told him, "Moving to Vermont won't get Mom and Dad out of your head." What I told him was true, but deep down I did not want him to move to Vermont to live with me.

I was about fourteen years old when I heard a knock on my bedroom door. I was in my nightgown and ready for bed. It was Matthew. He asked, "Melissa, can I see your boobs?" I really did not expect that question and thought he was just curious, so I lifted my nightgown. I thought that was the end of it. I was wrong. He kept after me, wanting to explore more. He was very persistent. Sometimes I would raise my voice so Mom or Dad could hear and that would send him away for a while. I felt torn. I was frustrated with Matthew, but I wanted to protect him at the same time. At one point I told Mom. She said that she would speak to Matthew about it, but she added, whatever I did "don't tell your dad."

She didn't have to say that; I didn't want to tell dad. Matthew and I would talk, and he would promise he was going to stop pursuing me. And then he would be after me again. I became fearful as he grew taller that I could not fight him off if he got forceful. I lived with that fear every day. All the while Matthew and I were struggling with this, no one knew he was mentally ill. With knowledge of his illness, and the fear he might resume his sexual pursuits, I did not want him living with me. After his death, however, I felt like I had abandoned Matthew myself by discouraging him from coming to Vermont.

I was overwhelmed, but I didn't know it. I have no idea what I was like to be around at that time. I was angry, deeply sad, and frustrated with the way things were. Everything seemed wrong. So I coped as I had learned to cope: I talked. I talked about Matthew to anyone who would listen. I also drank alcohol, but it did not relieve the pain. Yet, I knew on some subconscious level that I was not going to live at home in Ohio again, job or no job. That fear had been replaced by anger.

Working conditions continued to deteriorate at the nursing home. Short staffing was a chronic problem. It was not unusual to have one nurse, and two nurse's aides on a floor with forty or more people. Sometimes we were lucky enough to have an aide to float between floors. Still, this was not enough. The work was backbreaking. The people we cared for were neglected in all respects, and I started complaining to anyone who would listen. The day came when the tensions broke. I do not remember exactly how it all happened. Another aide, who was a friend, called me from the floor she was assigned and said, "I have had just about enough. How about you?"

All energies came together, and the next thing I knew, all of the nurse's aides went to the break room while the nurses stayed on their respective floors. Someone called the newspaper.

When the reporter walked into the break room, he said, "I hear there's a strike going on here." There was dead silence.

Finally someone spoke up. "I'm just taking my break. I'm not on strike." With that being said, I decided to talk to the reporter. As I spoke, others chimed in as well. The nursing director had a couple aides from the day shift come in so we would have more help that night. The reporter left, and we returned to work. The article was in the paper the next day.

A few weeks later, we were informed that the nursing home was being sold to a larger company. At this point I thought I understood. I thought that there must have been a hiring freeze due to the impending sale. I had high hopes for the new company and appointed myself advocate for the nurse's aides and for the people who needed our care. The new administrator and the assistant nursing director granted me a meeting. They listened to my grievances.

The administrator said, "I know—ice cream sundaes! We will have ice cream sundaes for all the employees." He looked at the assistant nursing director. "Will you take care of the details?" She agreed to do so, and the meeting ended. I left feeling defeated.

Shortly afterward, a table was placed in the break room. On it were all the fixings for ice cream sundaes. I stood with my coworkers as they gobbled their sundaes. Mine did not taste so sweet. Someone said to me, "Wasn't it nice of them to do this?" I don't remember my reply. Here I was trying to get the staff more help and more pay. I was hoping we would not have to work so hard, and the people who needed our help would receive more care, more often—and this is what we got instead. Worse yet, my peers thought it was great.

A few weeks later I was fired for not letting them know I was out of town when I called in sick. My world was spinning out of control, and at that point I didn't care where I landed. The nursing director, who was actually very kind during the firing process, allowed me time to say good-bye. I went room to room saying good-bye to the people I cared for so deeply. As I walked out of the nursing home door, I knew this journey had ended.

# PART 2

# A Time to Reflect

CHAPTER 5

# Everything Is All Right

On cold windy days the dampness and chill of the season would go right through me. On these mornings, Mom would turn up the heat before waking Matthew and me. I would lie in bed, listening to the low rumble of the furnace as it warmed up, and wait to hear the air blowing out of the registers. I would then jump out of bed, grab my pillow, and bolt to the register by the front entrance. I would place the pillow against the wall and lean on it. I sat over the register and enjoyed the warm blowing air. From this small space I could only see a portion of the living room. I would listen to Mom and Dad having a conversation in the kitchen as Matthew ran from room to room playing. In these moments

I felt safe and secure in my family, even more so than during holidays. I was content in my warmth as I observed my family.

All contentment seemed lost as I walked away from the nursing home. Why did no one see what I did? I felt my concern didn't matter. It didn't make sense to me. Why let these people continue to suffer? Why keep care providers pushed to their limit and refuse to see that they cannot meet the need? Why do so many people want to turn their heads and pretend this suffering does not exist? Why do we tuck our most vulnerable people away in a place that we want to believe will do their best to care for them, only to deny the neglect when we see it? Somewhere deep inside we know that those who suffer are us; and deny it as we may, their suffering affects us either directly or indirectly. Is this too painful to acknowledge?

Matthew also was ignored. His mental illness made him difficult to be around, even scary at times. Matthew told me he didn't like the medications that were given to him for his disease. He said these medicines made him feel dull. As much as we wanted to have the real Matthew present, he wanted it more than any of us. Thus began a cycle of on and off medications. There was no real help for Matthew. Our family was in turmoil and I ran away to Vermont. Family support was fleeting and unstable at best.

Our parents wanted to maintain an image and didn't want the neighbors to know our family struggles. Our neighbors, as well, didn't want us to know their problems. So there we were, all pretending. I hated it and didn't always keep quiet.

The pressure cooker inside Matthew reached its boiling point. He lived in a furnished efficiency apartment near the university where he was studying to become a naturalist. His behavior became erratic, and no one understood why. He drove to the town where my parents lived and bought a gun—at least this is what I was told. And then he drove for a long time. He was in emotional turmoil and had nowhere to go. He was angry at Dad. He pulled off the road near a corn field, placed the gun on his temple, and pulled the trigger. There he remained in his car until a passerby found him the next morning. His suicide note subtly indicated that he was thinking of killing more than just himself. Perhaps it was not the insane part of Matthew who committed suicide. On some level Matthew knew he might kill others, namely Dad. The true Matthew did not want to do this, so he stopped himself. I heard that the people who knew him at the university were surprised. Perhaps they wondered, "Where did this come from?" Perhaps it came from a family full of secrets that pretended publicly that all was well. If we don't acknowledge suffering, how can we fix it? Perhaps all these pretenses contribute to so much pain, neglect, and loneliness.

A deep sadness was settling in around me. Never did I cry so much as I did after Matthew's death. I was crying for his loneliness. I wanted to know that he was safe and loved. I wanted just one last chance to hug him and let him know that he was not alone. A couple of months after Matthew died, and shortly before I was fired, I was giving Marge a bed bath. She had become very ill and was in a coma. My mind was on Matthew and not on my work. I felt Marge's hand wrap around mine. Her eyes opened and she looked at me directly. She said, "Everything is all right the way it is." I was numb and said, "What?" She said again, firmly and strongly, "Everything is all right the way it is." Her hand released mine and she was nonresponsive again. My sadness was deep and it took a while for this moment to sink in.

I was angry that Matthew had no safe place to go. I was mad at myself that I had not let him come to Vermont. I was upset that I did not have a job, and I didn't know where to go from here. Yet on the outside I did not appear this way. I continued going out with my friends, drinking alcohol, and talking to anyone who would listen about Matthew and my family.

One night I had a dream. I heard the phone ring. I jumped out of bed and ran downstairs to answer it. It was

Matthew. His words were sharp. His voice was low. I could not understand what he said, but I felt his angry energy. I woke up. I was in Ohio for Christmas, the first one since his death. The dream disturbed me. Was he upset that I was there? Mom was angry, and she denied it, but I could see it in her eyes. Dad talked a lot. I could tell that his talking drove Mom crazy, but she said nothing. Grandma was also in the house. She was a quiet, accepting soul who had seen many losses. She was a grounding force in our house of hidden turmoil.

Grandma and I had a special bond. As a teenager I would spend the night with her at her senior citizen apartment complex. We would talk, cook, and play Scrabble, and I would poke around on her piano. She taught piano for many years, and occasionally she would teach me a few chords. I admired that she had remarried at the age of sixty-six to a man who was seventy-nine. He was the only grandfather Matthew and I knew. He died when I was twelve years old. Grandma told me that she had been happier during those nine years of marriage than she ever was with Mom's father. Grandma's quiet way of being drew me to her. She was a strong woman. Mom used to tell me how Grandma would go down to the basement to chop coal with an ax, load it into a bucket, and lug it upstairs to the stove. Now in her eighties, arthritis had distorted Grandma's back. Yet she still walked. She lived in a nursing home, as things had become too difficult for her to stay at her apartment. She did not want to live with any of her children. For her, the nursing home meant independence. At this point she was still fairly able and could speak for herself. These ingredients made her nursing home journey more tolerable. She was in constant pain but rarely showed it. When Matthew died she did not want to go to his funeral. I never knew why and did not ask. I know she loved Matthew. Perhaps she simply did not want to witness his burial. Perhaps she had seen enough pain in her life.

Matthew's absence on Christmas was palpable. Mom broke down during Christmas dinner. I was relieved to see her cry. She needed to release some of that pain. We were a family going through the motions. I was struggling between empathy and anger toward my parents. Feeling overwhelmed, I knew it was time for me to return to Vermont.

CHAPTER 6

# My Lost Years

Was my life ever ordinary? I wanted to find a safe and secure place with safe and secure people who cared about me. At that time I drew to me people in as much, or more, emotional pain as me. So there we were, all spinning around looking for something in each other which none of us had to offer. Instead of feeling safe, we felt fear. Instead of finding security, we created the opposite.

Initially facilities would not hire me after my termination from the nursing home. A day care center for children became my next place of employment. This led to me and a friend opening our own day care home. I moved to an apartment where I could live and operate the day care. I also stopped drinking alcohol and began attending AA meetings. The day care environment allowed me to see that there are many parallels between old people and children. Both are in need of care and direction. Both offer the purity of blunt honesty. Children are not yet weighed down and whittled away by the world. Old people have let the ways of the world go in many respects. Therefore, both offer a freshness of perspective. When children misbehave, I could give them a time out. Often I wished I could give old people a time out, since they misbehave too. Oh well, perhaps a little misbehavior is good for the soul.

Many of the choices I made during those years I regretted as soon as I put them into action. I was twenty-six years old and emotionally spinning. My tears for Matthew seemed endless. I became needy and moody. Sympathetic listeners were becoming more difficult to find. I was stuck in own my story, and some people became tired of hearing it. Matthew's last conversation with me haunted me. Eventually I decided to cut communication with my parents. I didn't want to stop talking to Mom, but I was afraid she would share our conversations with Dad, even though Dad said his anger was gone. I could not get some of the memories out of my mind.

A few weeks before Matthew's suicide, Dad called me at the nursing home. He told the nurses to tell me that Matthew was dead. At this point I knew Matthew was alive. I tried calming Dad down on the phone.

I said, "Dad, why are you doing this? I love you."

He said, "You're nothing but a selfish pig."

He kept calling the nursing home and asking for me. His voice was monotone. I kept saying that I loved him. I was torn between hurt, anger, and frustration. He continued to call me a selfish pig. Nothing I said would break through to stop the craziness. Finally, the nurse refused to give me the calls. In fact, she told him to stop calling, but he kept calling, trying to manipulate her by the tone of his voice. In all honesty, I don't remember exactly when the calls stopped that night. Supposedly he had disowned me during this time. It was this dad I wanted to get away from. It was this dad I was angry with after Matthew died. I was also upset with Mom for not being able to stop what was happening with Dad.

The previous few years had been too painful. I felt that I had no one to defend me. Matthew had no one either when he was alive. Despite these feelings, it was painful to cut contact with my parents. Perhaps I thought I would be able to find relief. Yet, it is easy to hold pain close to the heart. This pain, like a precious stone, I clung onto tightly. Perhaps the turmoil of the past became my unspoken connection to my parents. In my friendships I sought defenders. I let myself be influenced by people I hardly knew and let go of true friendships. Perhaps these new friendships created a subconscious diversion from my own reality. All that I really managed to create for myself at this time was loneliness. So I worked several jobs. At one point I was working five different jobs. I hung on to the day care when it would have been best to let it go; it simply did not provide enough income. During this time I became acquainted with assisted living facilities. Time had passed, and I was able to work with the elderly again. I liked the assisted living environment, but they were not without issue. There was too little staff at times, people were admitted who required more care than assisted living facilities were equipped to provide, and ultimately the other people living there were neglected. Yet, I saw some people thrive in these facilities. That was rewarding.

My relationship with my business partner at the day care deteriorated over the years. I wanted out but was afraid to make that decision. I was exhausted from working too much. I continued to wallow in my own trap. I missed my parents. As I worked with the elderly, I became increasingly aware that the people I was caring for were close to my parent's age. I did not want things to end this way.

I began to pray for resolution. I also made amends with people I had hurt, and I felt a great weight lift from me. Still I remained afraid to reach out to my parents. I continued to pray. I finally realized it was time to close the day care. I began that process as well.

Just before Easter in 1996 a card arrived at my address. It was from my parents. All these years they had been sending me letters at my business partner's address. I had used her address so I could continue to write to Grandma. I asked my business partner not to give me my parents' letters. I was afraid their words would pull me in emotionally. What a quandary—I missed them, I cared about them, and I was afraid of them. Now they were reaching out to me, and I was ready to reach back. As it turned out, they had hired a private detective to check on my well-being. He posed as a parent seeking childcare. I wasn't angry with them for this, yet I was relieved. My parents wrote in the card that they would be coming to Vermont in the fall. They hoped I would see them. I picked up the phone and called home. It had been ten years.

# PART 3

# A Time to Heal

## CHAPTER 7

# The Reconnection

The cold fall wind blew through my hair as I walked up to the motel where I had arranged to meet my parents. I shivered as the burgundy denim coat I wore was not warm enough, but it was the coat I wanted to wear for our reunion. I had arranged for a therapist to mediate. I felt we might need some guidance as we spoke face to face for the first time in ten years. I don't know if my parents thought it was necessary, but they went along with this plan anyway.

It was odd; my thoughts were optimistic as I entered the building when I usually tended to lean toward negative thinking. With cautious excitement I entered the room. Dad hugged me first. His hug was strong and firm. Mom's hug was more tentative. Our talk of the past was brief yet clear. I made amends for some things I had said in my good-bye letter to them. My parents acknowledged my pain as well. We said enough kindly and without judgment or expectation to begin the healing of our family. I held back my emotions as I tried to sort out my parents now from my parents of the past. I decided to trust them, at least for now. So the therapist left. He felt he was no longer needed. Mom, Dad, and I went to a restaurant for dinner. We were a family again.

Now reunited, we were beginning a new journey. I was also stepping into a new journey of my own in Vermont. I was climbing out from one of the loneliest times in my life. Feeling out of place was pretty much a constant for me. I remember as a child feeling envious of Matthew. He was outgoing and always seemed to have friends. I was afraid of rejection. As a result I would often let people pick me instead me of choosing my own friends. I always felt that I wasn't enough. When someone chose me, I knew at least I was enough for them. When I was eight or nine years old, a friend asked me to spend the night in the treehouse in her backyard. I loved that treehouse and had spent many hours playing there, but I had never spent the night. In the afternoon before the sleepover, I went to her house to ask her a question. When she answered the door she told me that she had decided to have another friend spend the night.

She said, "I know if anyone would understand it would be you." I pretended and said, "Of course it doesn't bother me. I understand." I didn't tell her how excited I had been about spending the night in the treehouse or that I felt crushed and hurt. Instead, I puffed myself up and pretended it was okay, at least until I got home. When I told Mom about it, she was mad and wanted to call the girl's mother. I asked Mom not to call. It was too late to fix it. In my mind I felt I was not good enough for her to want to spend that time with me. I carried this part of me everywhere, and as I was starting this new chapter in my life, I brought that part along as well. This quiet, subtle insecurity affected all of my decisions, but I didn't know it.

My parents stayed in Vermont for four days. I saw them between jobs. I think they wanted more time, but for me it was enough. My business partner did not want them coming to the day care, which meant I could not show them my home. I didn't argue with her about it, as I wanted the closing of this business to go as smoothly as possible. I was still guarded with my parents. They seemed to be softer and I wanted to embrace it, but I still held back. Yet, there was no question that we had a common goal of reconnecting. My parent void was filled. My life in Vermont was also changing. Change frightened me. Even though I was very lonely during the day care years, I was afraid of being even lonelier. I had not yet learned to make decisions when my mind was quiet and not fearful.

There is always something to be learned through making mistakes. During the day care years I found sobriety. This facilitated healing in many directions. I also gained business skills which prepared me for my next venture. However, many of my life's choices were not my own. If a suggestion seemed good, sometimes I ran with it. Such was the case this time when I started a home health care business with a new business partner. I became the seriously driven business person, and my business partner was the bubbly, outgoing promoter. This combination worked and a business was born from essentially nothing. Dad was not encouraging about it. He was not critical either. He mainly expressed concern about my financial security. In typical stubbornness I was determined to prove that this business could make it. I felt the time was right. There were not many home health services in the area, and the need was great. This was a risk worth taking. Everything seemed to be coming together. My life was full. I had a new home, new relationships, a better relationship with my parents than I had ever had, and a growing business. I was embracing this time with enthusiasm when during a seemingly routine call, Dad said," Honey, I saw the doctor yesterday, and I have been diagnosed with cancer."

# CHAPTER 8

# No Time

We could not heal our family brokenness with more brokenness. Mom, Dad, and I all wanted our family to work. My parents had done their personal work their way. They became involved with the Catholic Church again and talked to the priest about our separation. I put myself in and out of therapy and applied the twelve steps from AA to my life. We had taken different routes, but it led us to the same place. Our healing wasn't perfect. On my first visit home to Ohio after the separation, I let my guard down. Basically, I talked too much, too openly, and it brought out the controlling part of Dad. At first I was hurt and afraid that we would have to take distance again. I confronted him in a letter.

On my next visit home, Dad told me that he wasn't going to write me as much because I misinterpreted what he was trying to say. Mom was not around when he told me this. I felt that I wasn't misinterpreting anything, but I said nothing. Dad's interactions with me improved. I realized I could not share as openly as I would have liked to with him. I had to accept both parents as they were. There were qualities about me that bothered them. My parents had to accept these as well. This acceptance allowed us to be a family.

Now cancer was interrupting our family. Cancer was the death word. Fear and sadness overrode my other emotions. How could this be? I had just gotten my family back, and now Dad might be dying. However, it turned out that he wasn't dying. He had prostate cancer. The tumor was removed and he received radiation. Dad was free of cancer.

I settled into my new normal. I called my parents every Sunday and flew out to visit them in Ohio once or twice a year. I don't really like flying, but I enjoyed seeing them as they waited for me at the end of the terminal. I enjoyed our hugs upon my arrival. Prior to our reunion, hugs had been few and far between. Each time I visited I would find flowers in my bedroom and a card welcoming me home. I was grateful to have the feeling of home again. Visiting them became a reprieve for me from the stresses of running a business, even though I could never really get away from it. Home care is the kind of business that has a rhythm of its own. It ebbs and it flows. When we were busy, we couldn't find enough employees to cover all the clients. When we slowed down, we lost employees. It was a frustrating cycle. I learned the hard way many times. Yet, through these ups and downs we managed to establish ourselves in the community. It was a lot of pressure and a lot of vigilance. At points I became too focused on it.

It's funny how life has a way of distracting our focus. We often take everything for granted while assuming things will always remain the same and then we get slapped into reality when life suddenly changes. We often forget to value those we love and to spend valuable time with them now. Do not assume we can postpone these connections until sometime in the future, for they may not be there. It was frustrating to me. It's not like I had never had this lesson before. Perhaps I become too absorbed in my home life and my business. All seemed to be going well until Dad had a routine colonoscopy. As it happens all too frequently, the cancer had returned. This time Dad had non-Hodgkin lymphoma. He would not be free of cancer this time.

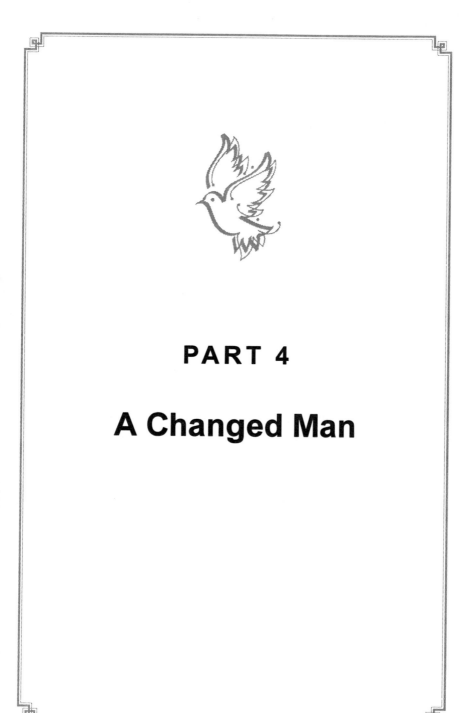

# PART 4

# A Changed Man

# CHAPTER 9

# A Complicated Man

"Look kids! Daddy's going to die!" Dad exclaimed. He grabbed his bottle of narcotics for stress and took out a pill and then he reached into the cabinet above the refrigerator where the liquor was stored and pulled down a bottle of vodka. He poured it into a large drinking glass. Holding the pill for Mom, Matthew, and me to see, he dramatically took the pill with the vodka. He had just gotten home from work and still had his suit and tie on. His skinny figure with suit tails flapping as he spun around in the kitchen seemed to add flare to his drama. I don't remember the exact sequence, but he kept taking the pills with the vodka, as if on a dare.

I was fifteen years old. I was home from school recovering from a tonsillectomy. Matthew was fourteen years old. Dad grabbed Ollie, our family cat who did not go outside, and threw him out the back door.

With a crazy look in his eyes Dad grasped a pill between his fingers and said, "Anyone tries to get Ollie, it means I will take another pill."

We all were crying. Mom was standing beside the kitchen table wringing her hands. Matthew ran down the short flight of stairs to the back door. Dad ran over and kicked him in the back. Matthew still ran outside to retrieve Ollie. I started to hyperventilate. Mom got me a paper bag. Dad was still yelling. No matter what any of us said, it was the wrong thing to Dad. He would just take another pill with the vodka. I started tasting something salty.

"I think my throat is bleeding," I said.

"Oh my God!" Dad exclaimed. "I forgot about your surgery."

And then it was over, just as quickly as it started.

This was a time when we never knew what would set Dad off. We all walked on egg shells. Most of these events would start in the kitchen, often during dinner. Usually we could tell when it was coming. Dad would lie on the couch in the living room for hours. He seemed unapproachable. He would play his music, usually 1940s and 1950s big bands and soloists. The music would be a little too loud, and some days the music would play until three or four in the morning. I couldn't sleep because the music was too loud and the tension in the house was too thick. Sometimes I would go into my parents' bedroom where Mom was sitting on the edge of their bed smoking. I would sit beside Mom sometimes and complain, but mostly I felt powerless. I wanted to sleep, but more than anything I wanted peace.

Occasionally Dad would smash glasses and say cutting remarks, and more than once he took pills with vodka. I remember being afraid to chew celery at the dinner table. I was afraid the crunching would set him off. Matthew did not tread carefully around Dad. Many of Dad's blowups began with a disagreement between him and my brother. Both Matthew and I wanted Mom to leave Dad. I became hyper vigilant. I knew every creak in the floor and how to avoid it. I would creep around the house and listen to Mom and Dad talking. If it was a pleasant conversation, I went to bed with hope. If it was tense, I would continue to listen, waiting for the explosion. Matthew did not handle it as I did. He went into his bedroom and simply stayed there.

A very deep anger was building inside me toward Dad. I set my sights on Vermont and kept telling Mom I was going to leave as soon as I could. I could not stand the home environment. Dad tried therapy, hypnotherapy, and lots of medications, and once he checked himself into the hospital. Still it did not get better at home. If he was in a good mood, I dreaded the bad mood that might be on its way. I loved Dad, but I did not like him during those years.

When Matthew's mental illness came to light, things at home got more complicated. I was in Vermont at college. I avoided going home as often as possible. Emotionally, however, I could not disconnect. Tense phone calls, demanding letters, and even my own thoughts would not relieve me from my family.

Matthew's suicide sent shock waves through each of us. The morning after Matthew's funeral I was awakened by Mom knocking on my bedroom door.

"Melissa, your dad's at it again," she said quietly.

I got up and went into the hallway. There was Dad walking up and down the stairs, yelling for Matthew. He went into Matthew's bedroom. He started pawing his bed. I wasn't sympathetic. I was ripped. I told Mom to call the ambulance and get him out of there. I was sick of Dad's drama. An ambulance came to the house. The EMTs convinced Dad to go to the hospital. Dad became agitated once he got to the hospital. Two security guards were sent to stand outside the doorway. The doctor asked me to leave the room because I was irritating the situation. I was too angry.

Mom promised me on the way to the hospital that she would have Dad committed against his will. I called Jason who had driven me from Vermont to Ohio for Matthew's funeral. Jason was my boyfriend at the time. Things had been so volatile at home prior to Matthew's death that I felt safer with a traveling companion. When I told my parents that I was coming with Jason instead of flying home, Dad told me he would bury Matthew before I arrived. Of course, he did not follow through with this threat. Jason ended up staying with Dick and his family. My parents would not welcome him in their home. Dick was Dad's best friend. They had met in college and ended up operating three record stores in Columbus. They had closed the stores in 1967. Dad went into education, and Dick went into retail. Our families were very close when Matthew and I were kids. Dick's kids were like another brother and sister to Matthew and me. I am sure Dick and his family wanted to avoid it, but often they were pulled into our family drama, as was the case this time. Dick and Jason met us at the hospital. Dick went into the hospital room with Mom, Dad, and the doctor. Jason and I sat in the waiting room. We waited a long time. Finally Dick emerged. He walked over to us, holding a key.

When I asked what was happening, Dick said, "Your parents went to lunch."

I couldn't believe it.

Dick added, "They knew you would be upset. They gave me the key so you can get your stuff from the house."

After this event Dad swore his anger was gone. My next visit home was Christmas. I pushed Dad emotionally as hard as I could. I wanted to find his anger line. He sobbed, but he did not rage. Still I did not believe him.

This deep-seated anger toward Dad along with so much emotional turmoil over Matthew's suicide all contributed toward my decision to cut ties with my parents. A part of me wanted to disappear. So I did my best to do so. Yet, at the same time, I was very conflicted with this decision. I was also too vulnerable to outside influences. I still had so much mistrust and hurt toward Dad. After all, this was the man who raged and criticized in an effort to control and keep his family. Dad's moods ruled the household. This was the man who wanted me home yet pushed me away. Once he had Mom and Matthew call me in Vermont to tell me that he would burn the house down if I didn't come home for Christmas. This did not make me want to come home. When I was twenty-five years old, he called the police in my town and reported me as a missing person. He would disown me and then send me postcards with hurtful words. He made my world feel out of control even when I was eight hundred miles away.

Yet this was also the man who would come into my bedroom when I was very young, after I was settled in for the night. He would sit on the edge of my bed and softly sing me a lullaby. He wrote Matthew and I short stories which he would read to us. We loved listening to him read. Matthew and I would eagerly wait for Dad to come home from work. Sometimes he would have a small gift for us.

I had a very serious lung infection when I was about five years old. It was Thanksgiving. Dick and his family were sharing the holiday with us. Playing with their kids was one of my favorite things to do as a child. Dad knew this, so he put up a child gate in the doorway so I could see the kids playing and be a part of it from a distance. He also bought me some little toys he knew I'd like and placed them on the nightstand within arm's reach so that I could play with them if I felt well enough. This man gave Matthew and I an appreciation for music. He taught us to be open-minded and fair. Sometimes when Mom was cleaning up after supper, Dad would gently grab her away from the sink and dance with her around the kitchen. She would smile and laugh. In these moments, we were happy.

After ten years of not seeing or talking to him, I found a much softer, kinder father. Occasionally the other Dad would peek through, but he managed to subdue himself. I watched his compassion for others grow through his work with the church. He began caring for some feral cats near their home, even though he was initially critical of my doing the same thing in Vermont. I observed him being thoughtful and more tolerant of views other than his own. In all honesty, I did not ever witness him rage again. Now this very complicated man had a new cancer. It was a lot to digest.

# CHAPTER 10

# Struggle to Accept

Dad wanted to set the stage. He wanted people to see him through the haze of his façade. People might have said, "Bob doesn't look well today. I wonder if he is ill."

Dad would have said, "I have been slightly ill, but I'm better now."

No details—the mystery remained. Mom stood by silently. Dad wanted to sculpt an image and design the response. He told Mom that he did not want people treating him differently, like a sick man. I found myself frustrated that Dad was not thinking of Mom's needs. She was bearing this burden on her own with only my support from Vermont. Yet, she rarely called me on her own. Dad was usually on the other line with her. Perhaps these were shades of the old Dad, but not quite. He encouraged her to call me on her own. She just wouldn't, unless he was in the hospital.

Yet, Dad was a very sick man. Maybe he believed his own self-made image. Perhaps it helped him cope. My parent's life became a constant cycle of x-rays, scans, blood tests, treatments, and waiting for the results. There is a fine balance to make sure the treatment that kills the cancer does not kill person. Dad believed in the medical profession. He also educated himself enough on his own disease to be a friendly challenge. He included me on his team of advisers. This pleased me. However, as a care provider, I have seen much suffering and watched Dad navigate the medical terrain with cautious optimism. I observed that his care providers liked him. I saw their empathy as his condition declined with each consecutive visit. I had empathy for them. It must be a tough job. I also had empathy for Dad, along with a whole other mixed bag of emotions. I felt concerned and protective toward Mom, who seemed to have too much on her plate.

Matthew was never forgotten. Even during Dad's illness, on significant days, my parents would cut flowers from their garden, poor jugs of water, and collect garden tools. They would put it all in the back of their car and drive to Matthew's gravesite to tend his headstone. When I went with them, I always felt a stillness in the air as we walked toward

Matthew's grave. Their grief was palpable. Even after so many years, Mom wore her sadness like a great weight. Dad would busy himself pulling weeds around the headstone.

"You know," I said in attempt to relieve their pain, "Matthew still loves you."

"I know," Mom said softly with an unbroken gaze toward his grave.

Dad's last visit to Matthew's grave was on a very hot day. His breathing was labored, even with the use of his portable oxygen tank. He forced himself to do his same routine. This time Matthew's flower vase in front of his headstone would not pull up. Dad was not strong enough. I tried to pull it up to no avail. I was concerned about Dad and suggested just laying flowers on Matthew's headstone.

"No," Dad insisted. "This cannot be. This isn't right."

He continued to struggle with the vase that would not release itself from the earth. It was painful to watch. I knew Dad's battle was not with the vase. Mom and I told Dad that we were going to put flowers on Susan's grave in the baby section. Susan was my older sister. She was born with a hole in her heart. She only lived four days. Such unspoken sadness my parents carried.

Susan's vase would not pull up either.

"Whatever you do, don't tell your dad this vase won't pull up," Mom said.

We both had visions of him struggling over Susan's grave as well. We laid the flowers on her grave and stood a while, contemplating the daughter my parents had only briefly known. We returned to Dad. He was sitting on the ground beside Matthew's headstone. He had surrendered. Perhaps this was Matthew's and Dad's last struggle on earth. Dad wanted to control the outcome, and Matthew said, "Not this time, Dad."

## CHAPTER 11

# Long-Distance Good-Bye

Ten years of struggling with cancer had taken its toll on Dad. When I came home in May 2008, I found a man who was losing the battle. The disease on the inside was showing itself on the outside. Dad had always stood upright with his shoulders squared. He had possessed an intense stare and looked people directly in the eye. Now his neck was bent so forward that he had trouble lifting his head to look at anyone. He had used a cane for the last couple years, but now he was dependent on it. He tried to straighten himself when I walked into the living room when I arrived home. Mom had picked me up at the airport since he was too sick to come. I was filled with deep sadness when I saw him, but I tried to cover it up. Dad was trying so hard to appear to be okay. The hum of the oxygen concentrator filled the house. When Dad walked, Mom would run around the house, trying to make sure the oxygen tubing didn't catch on anything. It looked to me like Mom had lost weight. I was concerned for both of them.

Less than two years before, Dad walked three times as fast as Mom. He was concerned that she was slowing down and that her shoulders had become so slumped. Though he had cancer then, it was not visible. He looked and acted healthy for the most part. In December 2006, he got pneumonia. He almost died. Shortly after that he had a blood clot in his shoulder, which was removed. He never really bounced back. Mom saw the worst of it at home. When they went out, Dad put on a good act. Now all pretenses were gone, but his determination was still strong.

The day after I returned home Dad had an appointment with his oncologist. His doctor understood that Dad still wanted to fight despite the fact that things seemed pretty hopeless. The doctor admitted him to the hospital.

Shades of the old Dad reappeared. He was resistant to most suggestions. He wanted to be in the hospital, yet he did not. Mom and I could not say anything right. We were all frustrated. This disease had its impact on all of us. The next day he was more vulnerable and less argumentative. Mom and I felt sad as we sat in the hospital room with him. Dad held up his arms, and the hospital gown sagged on his bony body.

"I'll be glad when this is over," he said. "This isn't quality."

Perhaps this was the first hint of surrender.

I said, "Maybe you will feel better at home."

He said, "I hope so." He sighed deeply.

When Dad was sent home, Mom and I had great reservations about it. At the same time, we wanted him to be where he was happy. He was still resistant to receiving nursing help at home. When we pulled into the driveway after his release from the hospital, Dad said, "I want to open the garage door."

By the time I got the portable oxygen tank out of the car, he looked at me and said breathlessly, "You open it."

By the time I got him into the house he was in respiratory crisis and in a panic to get to the bathroom. He began urinating before he reached the toilet. I had been fearful of crossing the line from daughter to care provider. For me it was quite different to care for a parent as opposed to someone unrelated. Thankfully, I found I could do it.

I helped Dad onto the toilet and was in the process of helping him change his underwear when Mom came in.

After he was cleaned up, we helped him into the living room. Much of my memories of Dad were in that living room—some were good and some were not. That is where he listened to his music. He had a chair next to the record player. Each day he spent hours in that chair, even when he was healthy. Now this was where he wanted to be. Mom and I would offer food, give him his medications, and help him to the bathroom. Sometimes we would just sit with him in anticipation of a few words between us before he would drift off to sleep, exhausted from just living.

That evening, Dad wanted to go upstairs to bed. He was resistant to a hospital bed downstairs. The couches in the living room were loveseats and not long enough to lie on. I followed him as he climbed up the stairs. However, Dad did not go up slowly. He grabbed the hand rail with determination and excelled up the staircase. About halfway up he told me it was okay to push. So I pushed. By the time he reached the top of the stairs, I was supporting almost all of his weight. He stumbled into the bedroom in respiratory distress, panting and moaning. He sat on the bed. Mom came in. I left the room feeling frustrated and angry. At this point I decided to confront Dad. I went back into their bedroom. I told Dad that he needed to get a hospital bed because there was no way Mom could support that much weight, as it was difficult for me.

Dad said breathlessly, "It might get better."

I said, with a knot in my stomach, "No, it's not, Dad."

I tried to soften the confrontation by saying I did not like seeing him this distressed. Well, Dad then informed me that I was the stressor. So I decided to leave their room. It bothered me that I was so angry at a dying man.

Mom told me that I must not love my father because I confronted him when he was so distressed. I explained that I had purposely done this. Dad did not recognize the problem when he was at rest. I was hoping he would recognize his needs while he was in the throes of it.

I had purchased a round-trip ticket. I had already paid a penalty for postponing my visit due to a cold, which I could not expose Dad to due to his chemotherapy. Circumstances indicated that I should stay. However, in many ways, Dad was right. I could be a stressor. My parents had their own system between themselves. I was powerless over it. In our family's history, so often Dad and I had gone nose to nose and toe to toe. I didn't have patience for his stubbornness, which often felt hurtful. However, now was not the time. I did not want Dad and I to end this way. It was best that I leave for a few days.

The next morning I talked to Dad about not putting himself into unnecessary respiratory distress and moving more slowly. That evening he climbed the stairs slowly, under his own power. This time he was not as distressed. He understood that Mom could not support his weight. We decided I should not change my airline ticket again. I would go back to Vermont with the understanding that I would return when they felt they needed me. I did this with great reservation. The night before I left, Dad got up multiple times, but he would not allow Mom or I to help him. I felt I was not contributing much by being there. I called a hospice organization and set up an appointment with them to visit my parents the day I returned to Vermont. My parents agreed to this plan. Even though Dad was still resistant to a hospital bed, he did agree to get a recliner.

A very kind neighbor gave me a ride to the airport. When she pulled into the driveway, I gave Mom a hug, and then I gave Dad a hug. We embraced hard and long. At that moment I felt Dad's love with every fiber of my being. I tried to hold back my tears. I did not want to discourage him. As we pulled out of the driveway, I could see my parents waving from the big picture window. Dad was leaning forward in his chair and waving with his right arm. I let the tears flow. I knew this might be the last time I saw him alive.

I was away for six days. I wanted to call them every day, but Dad did not think it was necessary, so I called as he specified. Dad had an appointment with his oncologist, but he was too weak to make it to the hospital for the appointment. The oncologist said he would make a home visit. I was impressed by this gesture. At this point Mom said that she would like me to return. Dad was still resistant.

"Why don't we see what the doctor says about my coming back?" I said. Dad agreed to this. I was already planning on flying out the next day. I knew Mom would not have asked for support if she didn't need it. Actually, she was beyond needing it.

I called my parents while the doctor was doing a home visit for Dad. The doctor said it was a matter of days until Dad died. I told him I was flying out the next day. He thought that was fine. I also asked him if he could convince Dad to accept a hospital bed, or at least convince him to stop going up and down the stairway. He said he would do his best. The doctor also told me that he had ordered home health nursing care for Dad. It was time to prepare for an extended stay in Ohio. I put myself into action mode, not feeling mode. This was the only way I could function.

It was about two in the afternoon. I had just pulled into the veterinarian's parking lot to pick up some cat food in preparation of my leaving. The receptionist from my office called to inform me that Mom was trying to reach me. When I called home my mother answered. She wanted to know if Dad should sign a Do Not Resuscitate form. She told me the nurses were there. She wanted me to speak to one of them and then gave the phone to the nurse, without waiting for my response. I told the nurse that Dad was hesitant about signing a DNR form. She told me that she felt Dad would be better off in a facility. At the same time she was afraid that he would not survive the transport. She wondered if Mom would accept the twenty-four-hour crisis care. I definitely wanted Mom to have that support, so I said "yes" for her. The nurse told me that Dad's oxygen stats were very low when she arrived and had dropped significantly since they had been there. This drop occurred while he was still on four liters of oxygen through a nasal cannula. I asked the nurse if he had a fever. It has been my experience that some people in a dying process run a fever. She said it was 99.5. For Dad this was high, as his normal temperature ran about 96.7. I felt strongly that Dad was actively dying. I asked the nurse if he could still speak. She said that he could and handed the phone to Dad. I could hear him struggling to speak. I asked him if he still did not want to be ventilated, even though I knew it would not help at this point.

He said, "No ventilator," as he struggled to speak.

I said, "Dad, do you know what is happening to you?"

He said, "I think so."

I said, "Dad, you may not be there when I get home."

He said, "I know." There was a pause and I could hear Dad struggling to breathe. Dad coughed and I could hear rattling in his chest.

"Dad, it sounds like you have a lot of fluid in your throat," I said, even though I knew it was the death rattle. I was overcome with emotion, but I was trying to suppress it for Dad.

He said, "It started last night," and then he whispered, "The doctor said three more days." He sounded so vulnerable.

I said softly, "We don't always have control over that."

Dad replied in almost whisper," I know."

Dad was really struggling to breathe. He was trying to tell me something about the doctor. He was frustrated that he could not get it out.

I said, "It's going to be okay, Dad"

This annoyed him and he said strongly, "I know it's going to be okay." I could hear him laboring to breathe.

I said, "Dad, there is a medicine that can help relieve the fluid in your throat. Can you ask the nurse for it?" As soon as I said this I realized that Dad could not ask. I corrected myself, "Dad, I will ask her."

There was a pause, and I could hear his struggling intensify. I wanted to comfort him.

"Dad, you know it is going to be all right." I was referring to his death.

He said clearly, "I know it is." I knew he understood what I meant.

"I love you, Dad."

He responded strongly, "I love you too." I knew he meant it. I also knew this would be the last time I would hear his voice say those words to me.

Dad's laboring was getting severe by now. I told Dad that I loved him again and asked him to hand the phone to the nurse. It took a while. He was struggling with the phone. The nurse eventually spoke. I asked her for the medicine for throat secretions; I couldn't think of its name.

She responded, "Atropine," and I affirmed. I heard the nurse ask Mom to get the hospice package. Shortly afterward, Mom got back on the phone. I told her that Dad was in the dying process. Things were now out of our hands. I asked Mom if she was okay with the crisis care.

To this she responded, "Do I have a choice?" And then she said in a softer manner, "I feel better with people here."

I told Mom I would call her soon. We hung up. So there I was sitting in my car in the veterinarian's parking lot, trying to sort out my emotions, as I knew I had just spoken to Dad for the last time. Sadness washed over me. I thought about Dad's voice. He had a strong, deep voice. I would miss his voice. The tears flowed. I felt so powerless. I sat in my car for a long time. Finally, I calmed down enough to drive.

As it would be Joe, one of Dad's friends from the church, had gone to my parent's house to prune some bushes. Two other friends from the church stopped by the house to talk to Joe. None of them knew what was happening inside. I don't know exactly how it happened, but they all ended up inside helping my parents. Upon the nurse's request they helped move Dad from his favorite chair to a recliner. When these nurses arrived, I am sure they were not expecting to be caring for a man so deeply entrenched in the dying process. Mom was running to and fro, getting items for the nurses as they tried to make Dad more comfortable. The house was more active than it had been in ages. At a time when quiet was desired, it was hectic.

Through the chaos of it all, Mom leaned over Dad closely and said softly, "Bob, you are a good man." And perhaps those words floated through the chaos and entered into the stillness where Dad now dwelled as he waited for his next journey.

I waited in Vermont. Death can happen at any moment. I have witnessed people die quickly who had the potential to live much longer. I have also witnessed people live longer than their prognosis would indicate. I had no idea how long Dad's dying process would take. About two hours after I returned to the office, Mom called.

She said "Melissa, it's over. Your dad is gone."

I said "Oh, Mom."

She said, "Oh, Melissa."

We were both silent for a while, absorbing the fact that the strong life presence I called Dad and she called Bob was now out of reach.

# PART 5

## A Woman Released

# CHAPTER 12

# New Ground

Yellow and white butterflies danced around Dad's coffin. They floated freely in the warm summer air without a care in the world. I was so engrossed in watching the butterflies that I didn't really hear Dad's graveside service. Perhaps these magical moths were Dad's way of subtly reminding us of the simple joy of being.

Since I arrived home for Dad's funeral, I noticed Mom was very unsteady on her feet. I was concerned, but she seemed annoyed when I express this concern. For so many years we had had Dad to talk about. This was new ground for both of us. We were both busy doing the things people do after a family member dies. There were lots of people around, but I knew that would change in time. The house felt different without Dad. Even when I returned home after ten years of separation, the house still felt familiar. Now it felt strange. There was a security for me when my parents had each other. The thought of Mom alone in the house scared the hell out of me. A few years ago Mom and I had talked about her moving to Vermont when Dad died. Now faced with the reality of it, she did not want to leave.

Also, I had seen glimpses of a different Mom shortly before Dad died. One evening while Dad was in the hospital, Mom burst out to me, "You know, I can get your Dad to do things!" She paused and then added, "All I have to do is say, Bob, you can't do that, and he will be determined to do it." Her eyes flashed with an intensity I had not seen before.

It was the energy in how she said it that threw me. Her eyes glared with determination and anger. I wanted to say to Dad, "Who is this woman you are leaving me with?" This was about the time when Mom and I were frustrated with Dad because he wanted to return home without home health care services. We were torn between anger and empathy. This was a difficult time for all of us. Mom had always been the quiet one. Often she took the backseat, but fifty-three years of doing this had taken its toll.

Dick and Dad had hired Mom to work at their record store near the OSU campus. Dad had been engaged to another woman. This woman broke off their engagement when he would not close the record store to attend their wedding rehearsal dinner. When Mom realized the engagement had ended, I think she set her sights on him. She said that Dad was fun to be around. However, Dick and Dad had a business agreement not to date their employees. So when Dick went on a vacation, Dad asked Mom out. He proposed to her that very night over a milkshake. Mom agreed and three weeks later they were married. It was a very small wedding. Even though Dick was initially upset, he was the best man.

Dad did not like the dress Mom had picked out for the wedding. Thus the cycle began. Mom wanted to marry Dad, but she wanted a larger wedding. She also wanted to wait and not marry so quickly. It hurt her feelings that he did not like her dress. After they were married, Dick and Dad decided it was best for her not to work at the record store. She loved working at the store. She loved music and interacting with people who shared her interest. Little pieces of herself had been compromised over and over again.

Fifty-three years of being quiet for the sake of peace had worn Mom out. However, she wasn't always quiet. They did argue, but Mom often relented. Long before Dad died, the years of hurt had reached a boiling point. The steam burst out mostly in the evenings. Mom's mood would deteriorate. Even her face would show it. Mom and I always had our best conversations in the morning at the kitchen table. These moments with her were a highlight during my visits home. I looked forward to our mornings together. I know Mom did as well. I noticed the evenings had become increasingly difficult for her. She was tired and I began questioning how well she was even before Dad died. Dad and I had even talked about it. He shared my concerns.

Before I returned to Vermont, I set Mom up just like I would a client for my home health care business. We got a medical alert system. I put phones on every floor, placing them in the rooms she frequented the most. We made extra keys which we gave to trusted neighbors and friends. I talked to these people about my concerns for her safety. I got the phone numbers of the people who could check on her, and they got my numbers. Mom thought I was being overprotective. I told her it made me feel better. In all honesty, it did. Sure enough, I had not even arrived home from the Burlington airport when my cell phone rang.

"Melissa?" Mom said. Her voice sounded tentative. "I don't want you to worry, but I fell at the restaurant after church. My hand is turning black and it hurts a lot. So I am going to the emergency room to get it checked."

Everything was set to go, and Mom and I were already off to the races.

# CHAPTER 13

# A Need to Be Home

My parents were married for fifty-three and a half years, and for Mom that meant too many years of waiting for things to get better. During the last twenty years of their marriage, Dad was a much kinder and gentler man. At least that was what I observed. I often wondered if Mom couldn't get enough distance from him to see that he had changed. Their marriage during those years had settled into a calm routine. Now it appeared that Mom had changed. She needed someone to talk to. The hurt and anger of a difficult marriage still remained an open wound for her. I became that someone for Mom to talk to, and I realized how much hurt she had kept inside for all those years of their marriage.

She wanted to have fun. Dad was controlling, even somewhat to the end. So Mom developed ways of getting around that control over the years, but now she had no need to hide anything. Now feeling free, she ate a lot of ice cream, not ice milk or frozen yogurt—she enjoyed the real stuff. She went out to eat whenever she wanted, and she changed several pieces of furniture in the house. She began updating the house itself. She had me help hang pictures on the living room wall. She and Dad could never agree on which pictures to put up after the room was painted. Thus the walls had remained bare for fifteen years.

Mom traveled with me to Vermont. She also flew to Texas with one of my cousins. She greatly enjoyed the company of family in that region of the country. She continued to go to church on Saturday evenings and then out to dinner with friends from the church. She made friends quickly and easily. People liked her. They did not get the chance to really know her when Dad was alive. He didn't want to be social.

Mom and I talked to each other on the phone just about every day. It was comforting for me to hear her voice. We laughed, made plans, and even argued sometimes, but I loved our conversations.

For Mom it was one health problem after another from the get-go. She had lots of doctor appointments. Yet, her problems weren't life-threatening. The unsteadiness on her feet was a constant concern for me. If she didn't answer the phone when I called, I always pictured the worst-case scenario. Finally she hired a housekeeper who became a friend. I was glad for both. Mom continued to move slowly. Occasionally she needed help, but she didn't want to acknowledge it.

One afternoon Mom called me. It was unusual for her to call in the afternoon. We usually spoke in the evenings.

"Melissa, I don't want you to worry." I had learned to dread that statement. "But I have been diagnosed with colon cancer." Such news fell on me hard. I broke down. It had been just over a year since Dad had died. I knew that cancer might not mean an immediate death, since Dad had lived for ten years, struggling with three different kinds of cancer. In all honesty I didn't know which scares me more: the cancer or the treatment. I just knew that I did not want Mom to suffer. I wanted her to have a life of quality as long as she possibly could. Mom decided to get a second opinion. Yet, with a new hope of different news, we were again disappointed. The colon cancer was confirmed, and in addition, it was in a difficult location, which made surgery risky and difficult. Cancer was also in her liver. I felt that harsh treatments would be too much for Mom to handle. She agreed. Yet, she told me that she felt she had to do something. Mom didn't feel comfortable just doing nothing.

Mom chose to receive cancer treatments from the same hospital that treated Dad. She had a different oncologist. This doctor listened to our concerns and agreed that an oral, low-dose treatment of chemotherapy would be the best course to take. I flew out to Ohio to be with Mom for her first treatment.

I was glad I went home. Mom didn't react well to the treatment. Her joints ached so much that she could barely move. I could not leave until this issue was resolved. There was no way she could stay at home alone, even with the support of her friends. Apparently her joints had reacted to the treatment. The doctor ordered steroids. I extended my stay until she was able to better move around.

Sickness seemed to permeate my life. Mom was sick, the clients who chose my home care service were often sick, and even some of my animals were sick. I was sick of sick, but I was trying to hold it together. Sometimes I didn't do this so well. It was a balancing act. The saying "Take care of the care provider" is true. I have seen so many care providers push themselves too hard. This can result in sickness and sometimes death. Did the ten years of being with Dad as he dealt with cancer have such a negative impact on Mom that she now had cancer? I wondered if she had had the cancer while Dad was still alive. What impact did fifty-three years of hurt feelings have on Mom's disease? I knew I had to take care of myself so I could be available for Mom, as well as for my business. Some days I did this well, and some days I didn't.

Mom was constantly on my mind. I didn't want her life to deteriorate to a continual stream of medical visits. We decided on quality, with the hope that quantity would also happen. Some quality did happen. She was able to continue her life somewhat as it was before she was diagnosed. However, she got tired, especially after her treatments. Our conversations revolved around doctor visits, medications, and any other problems she might be experiencing. For several years Mom volunteered for an organization in which she read to blind people over the radio. When Dad was alive, they put together musical programs for this radio station. Mom truly enjoyed volunteering for this service, but she had to give it up.

Despite all of her losses, she had a way of being which I admired. She would take things day by day. If it was a good day, she enjoyed it. If it was a bad day, she just waited for the next.

Relaxation was not an option for me at this time. For so many years Mom had given herself up to Dad's wishes. Often she waited too long to speak her mind. Now waiting to speak wasn't an option. It required vigilance to make sure Mom was getting the correct care and to constantly monitor her condition. She was in no shape to do this on her own. In addition to her other side effects, her memory was being affected by the treatment. Both of my parents had a change of oncologists during the course their treatment. In both cases the doctors relocated to other areas. Her most recent oncologist would joke, "You look like you are fifty," and then he would add, "But on the inside you are not so good." Mom enjoyed his comment and would repeat it to her friends.

About a year after Mom's cancer diagnosis, this doctor told her that no more could be done and there was no point doing anymore treatments. No more treatments meant not much time. I felt an urgency to get home fast. I didn't tell Mom I felt this way. This not-so-quiet nudge from my inner voice needed to be heeded, and I flew home.

# PART 6

# Twenty Days for Charlotte

CHAPTER 14

# Night at the ER

I strongly dislike flying. Often when I flew out to or back from Ohio, I would run into difficulties at the airport. This time there was someone pointing me in the direction I should go when any uncertainties arose. The flight went very smoothly, but I hardly knew it. My mind was consumed with thoughts of Mom.

I will never forget the look on Mom's face as she looked at me through the passenger window when the car pulled up to the curb to pick me up at Port Columbus. This was the first time she was too sick to drive. A friend from church had kindly given her a ride. She was smiling. Her face looked so soft and fragile. I opened the passenger-side door and hugged her tightly, knowing that our hugs may be limited.

For the last couple of months Mom had a persistent cough. It didn't make sense to me. Why was her cough so severe when Dad had all sorts of issues with his lungs and he didn't cough? Scans indicated that Mom had some cancer in her lungs, but very little. Perhaps the cough was her body's way of trying to get rid of that cancer. On my first evening home we went to a new restaurant in town. We always enjoyed going out to eat together. This time, however, she was unable to control her coughing. She felt embarrassed. We asked for to-go boxes and left.

Mom went to bed that night hoping to awake the next morning with a diminished cough. I hoped for the same. Our hopes were dashed as she continued to cough throughout the night. We ate breakfast, but she was too tired to sit at the kitchen table and talk as we usually did. We went into the living room. This room, owned by Dad for so many years, Mom had claimed. Years of familiar had been transformed by new things—Mom's favorite being a leather reclining chair which she positioned so she could look out the big picture window. I sat on the couch in front of the window and drank my coffee, hoping we could talk. We did but only for short time. She was tired. This was the first of many long days.

Mom had an appointment with her primary physician the next day. This physician was wonderful to Mom. She always took time to answer any questions, and I could tell she genuinely cared about Mom. That night we went to bed with hopes that this doctor might have some solutions for Mom's cough. Mom had already taken several medications to no avail. Perhaps it was easier for us to focus on the cough than the cancer. There could be no quality as long as she was suffering with this intense cough. We were actually hoping it might be pneumonia. At least pneumonia could be treated.

The primary physician wanted Mom to get a chest x-ray and perhaps IV antibiotics, if the x-ray showed that she had pneumonia. This meant we had to go to the emergency room. The doctor offered an ambulance transport. Mom and I decided to go home first so we could feed the cats and prepare for a long night.

I dreaded going to the emergency room. Through my years in health care I had seen too much. Again, the issue of too much need, with not enough help, raises its head. There is the occasional time when an ER visit goes smoothly. That is what I was hoping for. We opted to go to the emergency room closest to the house in case I needed to return home to care for the cats. When we arrived, it was standing room only. However, Mom was too sick to stand for too long. We found seats and then we went into triage. Once we were finished in triage, we found an adjacent room which had fewer people. We sat silently with strangers, each glancing at the other, waiting for our name to be called so at least the waiting would end. We sat a long time. Mom convinced her friend who had given us a ride to the emergency room to go home. She was more than willing to wait, but we knew this might be an all-night affair. We would call when we were done. Mom was increasingly uncomfortable.

I approached the receptionist and asked, "How long?"

"I'm sorry," she said with compassion. "I am truly sorry, but unfortunately, your mom is not a priority. If someone comes in with a greater need, she will be pushed back."

Anger rose up within me. Mom was suffering. Anyone could see it. Was it her age that made her comfort not a priority?

"Apparently, you're not a priority," I muttered to Mom.

We waited some more. Finally, we were taken to a room. Well, perhaps the word "room" wasn't the right description. It was a space with curtains which was equipped like an emergency room. I helped Mom into her gown and helped her sit on the narrow bed. The nurse had trouble getting the IV line going. After many pokes into Mom's arm, another nurse was called to the room. She got the line running. I recognized that the staff was stressed. I would be too. We kept telling various ER personnel that Mom had cancer and we were concerned about the cough. This information was entered in the computer. There was very little eye contact, just a glance occasionally when the person typing would look up. People around us were always in a hurry, asking the same questions over and over again. Mom had a chest x-ray, blood work, and a urine test. The hours passed.

Eventually we were informed that Mom had a severe urinary tract infection. They wanted to admit her for IV antibiotics. There was no mention of the cancer or her cough. Mom was so tired. She thought maybe she should stay, so the nurse started the IV antibiotic.

"Look," said Mom a few minutes later. She held up her arm. It was twice its original size.

I rang for the nurse. I suspected Mom's arm might be infused. When the nurse came in she agreed, and the IV line was moved to Mom's other arm. I was concerned that the antibiotic had infused her arm. I was aware that some medicines can create tissue damage. I questioned the nurse about this. The nurse thought it was the IV fluids that infused Mom's arm. After everyone left I sat down beside Mom and felt relieved. Regular IV fluids might be uncomfortable, but they would not create long-lasting damage.

I watched Mom as she lay on the small ER bed. I was still unsettled about the whole ordeal. Feeling restless, I walked over to the IV bags. Her fluids were dripping normally.

There was a green bag over the antibiotic bag to protect the medicine from light. I lifted the green bag to observe the antibiotic drip. The bag was empty!

Now I was mad. I was also concerned about Mom's arm. I rang for the nurse again. When she came in, I showed her the empty bag. This time she said that the antibiotic had probably infused her arm. I explained my concerns, but she said it should be fine. And then we were alone again. I looked at Mom with her arms all bruised from multiple attempts to get an IV line going. One arm was now larger than the other, she was still coughing, and she still had cancer. Even though she was exhausted, she was also mad. Sometimes when Mom got mad it was difficult for me to differentiate who she was angry with.

I said," Mom, are you mad at me?"

She said through gritted teeth, "No, I'm mad at them!" She kicked the sheets.

I have always been able to hear things well at a distance. As I sat beside Mom, behind the closed curtains listening to the voices and sounds of the emergency room, I overheard a conversation.

"Do you think that it could hurt her?" I heard a woman say.

"I don't think so," said a male voice tentatively.

I am not sure they were talking about my mother, but the uncertainty was enough to raise my concerns again. I rang and asked to speak with the doctor. I am sure by this time they were tired of me ringing the bell. When the ER doctor came in to see Mom the first time, she looked drained. Her face appeared drawn, as if she had seen too much sickness and had too many decisions to make quickly. I felt empathy for her knowing that she was overburdened. I am sure this issue with Mom was just another burden on her plate.

Mom decided that she should go home instead of being admitted. She wanted an oral antibiotic to take at home. Having a UTI did not alarm her. She had dealt with this type of infection frequently over the years. In this facility, however, she felt unimportant.

A new doctor presented himself through the curtain. He was the admitting doctor. He informed us that if Mom stayed she would remain in the room she was currently occupying. I knew this meant very little help for Mom. She had not been checked on by the staff unless I rang. Mom couldn't call for help. She was too sick to do so. We told the doctor that we wanted to leave. He said if we did that, we would be going against doctor's orders. So I told him about the multiple bruises on Mom's arms, the IV infusion of the antibiotic, and the nurse saying it wasn't the antibiotic. When the empty bag was pointed out, she said it was the antibiotic. We stressed that we felt Mom was not well attended. All we wanted was an oral antibiotic for the UTI and to go home. We assured the doctor that we would call her oncologist in the morning. However, it was already morning.

The doctor's tone changed. He said he would ask the ER doctor to come in to talk with us. She had not yet come in after I had requested to talk to her. We waited some more. Suddenly, our nurse and another nurse burst through the curtains.

"It's all set. You can go home now," the other nurse said in a singing song voice.

Mom shot her a look and said, "You are being condescending."

I don't remember the nurse's exact response, but they sat Mom up. Mom's nurse took out the IV line. Mom's arm started bleeding. Mom was sputtering angrily. The nurse began to cry. I understood Mom's anger. I also understood that this nurse was having a very bad night. I had empathy for her as well. The next thing we knew, Mom was dressed and in a wheelchair, with discharge papers and a prescription for an antibiotic. As I wheeled her out of the emergency room I promised her that we would not come back. It was after six in the morning. We called a couple from Mom's church who graciously picked us up and brought us home. Mom went upstairs to lie down. I fell onto the couch—another day gone.

I just wished that someone working in that emergency room had enough time, or enough compassion, to recognize Mom's suffering and then say to her, "I am so sorry you have cancer. I am sorry you are so uncomfortable. We will do our best to help you." That compassion alone could have made a long night at a busy ER much more tolerable for everyone.

CHAPTER 15

# Memories and Mourning Doves

Each day I lost a little bit more of Mom. Our conversations became shorter. Friends came and went, but Mom was unable to enjoy their visits for any length of time. I took walks as a reprieve. It was still safe to leave her alone in the house for short periods of time. Ten days after my arrival, it was my birthday. That morning Mom got out of bed and came to the bedroom door. She said happy birthday to me in an out-of-breath kind of way. She went downstairs, took a direct beeline to her favorite chair, and fell into it exhausted. I made tea for her and coffee for me and brought them into the living room. She told me that my gifts were in a bag beside her bed upstairs. I brought the gifts downstairs. They were in a shopping bag. This was very unlike Mom. She always gift wrapped nicely and added special decorations. I could tell she was already getting tired. She was having difficulty staying awake. I pulled the unwrapped gifts out of the bag. She gave me an outfit: white capris, a black summer top, and a matching white jacket. Then I open the card. Mom told me as I opened it that she was too tired to shop for a card so she found a Valentine card I had sent her that she really liked and wrote a birthday note on that card. I was filled with deep sadness, but I tried not to show it. I knew this was the absolute best she could do at this time. I gave her a hug, thanked her for the gifts, and told her I loved her. I left the room so she could sleep, and then I allowed myself to cry. I knew that these were the last presents I would receive from Mom. It was the last birthday I would spend with her alive.

Later that afternoon some very close friends came by to visit. We tried to make light of the day. Mom was very pleased to see them. I was grateful they had come as well. We all knew our time with her was limited. We all pretended, in a way, like Mom wasn't dying. This was just a typical visit. Yet, when it was time to say good-bye, no one really had the words. Their love for Mom was conveyed through the final hug, look, or squeeze of her arm. Thus my birthday with Mom was almost over. Significant days often bring departures. Relief set in. This fear had haunted me all day.

Mom did not die on my birthday. However, Matthew's and Grandma's birthdays were only a few days away.

Elvis Pressley died on my twentieth birthday. I was sure at that time that half of my life was over. The age of forty seemed far away and ancient to me. That year I had stayed on campus to attend summer courses. As was the routine then, I called home. My parents had mailed some presents, and they wished me happy birthday over the phone. These were stressful years for our family. Matthew had joined the navy, only to be discharged a year later with the diagnosis of paranoid schizophrenia. Dad was unpredictable, and Mom just tried to survive the storm. I do not remember our conversation that birthday, but the family tension must have come through during the phone call because I was upset once the call ended.

I was living in a dorm suite with two of my friends from college. I went into my room and sat on the bed. One of my friends came in. She sat beside me. Anyone who knew me fairly well then was also aware of my family dynamics. I was not one to keep quiet about it. I started crying. We talked about whatever had upset me at the time and then we fell silent. She began touching me in ways no other woman had touched me before. It felt comforting. It felt right. We held each other all night. That was one of those moments for me when everything made sense. That was why I was not excited about dating men. I dated men because that was the norm. Yet, I was never comfortable with it. It felt like a chore or an obligation. Until that point, I had not thought of myself this way. I could be incredibly naïve. I felt complete. My friend, however, informed me the next morning that nothing could come of it. Over the next few weeks we still got together, but it wasn't the same. A door had opened for me, and now I did not know how to fill it. Over the next thirty years, I entered into relationships with women who did not want to commit as well as some relationships with men in an attempt to feel accepted socially.

I did not tell my parents about this part of me until I was forty years old. Once we had reconnected, I did not want to lie, cover up, or pretend with them anymore. They told me they weren't surprised. Shortly afterward, I received a letter from Dad saying he was concerned for my immortal soul. Mom said very little, as usual. This part of me created tension between us. However, it wasn't the elephant in the room that no one acknowledged. We did talk about it on my visits. I guess I was trying to make them understand me. It was a futile attempt; it is difficult to understand unless it is a part of you as well. Perhaps I just wanted their unconditional acceptance.

Yet, there was acceptance. They didn't condemn or alienate me. They didn't even criticize me. About a year before Dad died, while we were having our evening tea in the den, which was routine when I visited, Dad said something unexpected. I was talking to them about moving back to Ohio. I was discouraged with my life in Vermont. I asked them if they could deal with me dating women.

Dad said, "When I was in the hospital with pneumonia, I saw myself lying on the hospital bed."

Mom said, "Bob, you never told me that before."

Dad leaned back on the couch and said, "Well, I was hovering over my body and I was thinking, *What is my brain doing to me now?*"

I thought to myself, *It wasn't Dad's brain. It was his spirit.* However, I said nothing.

And then Dad said, "Anyway, after that experience, I realized that it doesn't matter."

I said, "So if I dated a woman here, it wouldn't bother you?"

Dad said firmly, "No, it wouldn't bother me at all." Mom said nothing.

I guess I assumed Mom's silence on many things meant approval. I was wrong. Even before Dad died she let me know that she accepted that part of my life, but she wished it were different. Mom explained that she was concerned about prejudice. Also, I think it would have been comforting for her to know I was in a marriage with a man. When she became ill, she became irritated any time the subject came up. I told her I wasn't going to talk to her about it anymore. Mom was sick. I didn't want that negative energy between us. She was full of hurt and anger that had nothing to do with me. I wanted to avoid a channel in which all that emotion could be directed at me. Yet, it hurt. I hoped that she would eventually truly accept me.

A couple days after my birthday, Mom had a final visit with her oncologist. He was very kind. He told her that she had done everything right, but there was nothing else he could do. He ordered hospice services. Her persistent cough, he felt, was the cancer. Mom had officially received her death sentence. I do not know how I would respond to such news. She was mad. A friend had driven us to the appointment. On the way home Mom sat in the backseat, scowling. We decided to stop at one of her favorite restaurants. She scowled through the meal. Her friend and I didn't know what to say. Mom eventually became too tired to be mad, and we went home.

I did not want Mom to die with all that anger. I encouraged her to talk about it. I told her that if she did not feel comfortable talking about it with me to find someone else she trusted. She decided to talk to her priest. However, he wasn't available, so another priest came to the house. I left the room so they could talk in privacy.

Mom still talked to me when she was able. Sometimes I was uncomfortable with the things she shared. Being her daughter, it felt awkward for me. So much emotional poison spilled out of my mother. It's funny I can feel so empathetic toward a stranger or someone needing care, but I had difficulty feeling the same toward my parents. I felt sad, frustrated, and even angry sometimes, but I did not know how to offer Mom my empathy.

Even before Mom began talking to me in this manner I understood that she had plenty to be upset about. I also had come to understand the foundation for some of Dad's hurtful behavior. Dick said that my father's mom was crazy. From the stories Dad told me, I think there was a lot of craziness in his family. That craziness drove his father away when Dad was an infant. His mother wanted a baby girl, not a boy, so she refused to cut his hair. He had very curly hair that bushed out. Dad's family lived in southern Ohio. His family ran an apple orchard. The farmhands taunted Dad about his hair. He was embarrassed even at such a young age. Sometimes when he and his mom went shopping in Huntington, West Virginia, she would park on the street and look for handicapped people. She would laugh hysterically at them while Dad sat beside her in the car. Another time, while they were shopping in West Virginia, she suddenly jumped in front of a moving car in an attempt to kill herself.

Mom never met Dad's mom. She died at the age of forty-four shortly after Dad had graduated from college. She was a schoolteacher. While she was watching the children during recess, a blood clot killed her right on the playground in front of the kids. At least, this is what I was told. Dad's emotional pain rebounded onto Mom. She did not know where it came from or how to handle it. She often told me that her family wasn't that way. My parent's first big argument happened three weeks after their marriage. Mom said Dad sat in a chair after that argument, staring at nothing for hours. From that moment on Mom began waiting for things to get better.

Perhaps she thought when Dad died she would have her opportunity to live as she wished. Now cancer had taken that chance away. It wasn't fair. Even before the cancer was diagnosed, Mom had problems. Still, any time I mentioned my concerns for her, she got irritated. She particularly didn't like me walking beside her in a protective manner. I couldn't help it. It was the care provider in me. However, I went against my gut, gave her the distance she requested, and prayed she wouldn't fall. Why is it when the truth is pointed out people get irritated? I have always had the wonderful knack of irritating the people around me.

Days became very long. Mom stopped going to the kitchen for breakfast. She stayed in her favorite chair most of the day. I brought food to her. Hospice services had started, and a hospital bed was set up in the living room. Mom had become too weak to make it upstairs. I also noticed that her legs were filling with fluid. Even though she was hesitant about taking morphine, it was the only drug that stopped her cough. Unfortunately, it knocked her out. I hoped when she awoke that she would have some peace, but she always woke up in a torrent of horrible coughing. I did not opt for hospice volunteers. Her friends from church were providing so much needed support. In fact, their support was very instrumental in Mom's ability to stay at home alone even prior to her diagnosis. I am so grateful for these people who gave to us so freely.

Yet, even with this support, I felt alone. There was no family nearby. Calls from my friends in Vermont helped. I was trying to find acceptance as I watched all that was familiar about home fade away. Now I would sit on the couch, drinking my coffee and watching Mom in a morphine-induced sleep. Once she woke up and saw me crying.

She asked, "Why are you crying?"

My throat tightened as I said, "Mom, I am watching you fade away." She looked at me, said nothing, and closed her eyes to sleep again.

In the afternoons when Mom was asleep I would sit on the back patio. It was a very dry summer in Ohio, but it made time on the patio pleasant; it was a quiet reprieve.

The patio was a place where we, as a family, often spent time. I remember Matthew sitting there, cupping his hands over his mouth and making the sound of a mourning dove. The mourning doves would call back to him. This space, for the most part, had peaceful memories. It was a place for conversation or just being quiet. Now it was a space for me to breathe. As I sat, I thought, "This is one of the hardest times of my life." Until that point I felt that the hardest thing I had ever done was walk up to Matthew's casket. At twenty-six years of age, death was new to me. As I approached the casket, Matthew did not look too different than in life, until I got closer. He had been placed in the casket with the bullet wound facing the wall. Most of that side of his face was blown away by the bullet. The morticians had filled the hole with black wax. I thought, *Why couldn't they have used skin-colored wax instead?* It would have made it easier, at least for me. Yet, I had requested to see his body. Having worked at the nursing home, it wasn't my first experience with death. But this was my brother. I was not emotionally prepared. I thought seeing his body would help me accept his death. I was afraid if I did not do this, then I would constantly be expecting him to walk around the corner. That night, as I tried to sleep, I kept seeing Matthew's face with the black wax. It would appear far away and then it would enlarge as it got closer. This happened over and over again. By morning I had no doubt that Matthew was gone.

Things were different with Mom, but equally difficult. I hated seeing her suffer. All of the experience I had through my years of caring for people was being put to the test. It was difficult for me to get a clear perspective. I was trying to give the best care to Mom and also take care of myself. I knew if I didn't take care of myself, then I wouldn't care for her well. I questioned myself every step of the way. Mom was so uncomfortable. I felt so powerless. I wanted to offer her hope, but it was hard to find. I was also getting tired. Sleep had become allusive to me.

While I sat on the patio mauling all these thoughts over, I observed a monarch butterfly. It floated around the corner of the house, sailing up and down in the light summer breeze. It floated until it was right beside me and then it flew straight up into the air and over the electric line on which a single mourning dove perched. The mourning dove made no sound. It simply watched me looking at it. Suddenly, another mourning dove flew from the roof of the house and attempted to perch next to the one on the electrical line. There was a fuss, and the first mourning dove shoed the second dove away.

I imagined that the dove on the line was Matthew and the second dove was Dad wanting to help. Matthew shoed

Dad away saying, "It's all right, Dad. I got this." Ever since Matthew died, mourning doves have a way of appearing during significant times in my life. Perhaps he was waiting for Mom, but for now he was supporting me. It gave me comfort knowing I was not alone. So there we stayed, the mourning dove and I, on that hot summer afternoon, enjoying each other's presence, until I heard Mom call for me. I went back inside to help her.

# CHAPTER 16

# Mom's Last Stand

Mom slammed her right hand on the arm of the chair and exclaimed, "Dammit, I'm dying!" Our visitors in the living room all shot me a look as if to say, "What just happened?" Actually, Mom was having a good moment. She wasn't coughing and she was communicating. She was tired of people dancing around the subject. She had talked to me about this a few times. What struck me the most about Mom at this moment was how much she looked like Grandma. She was wearing a long blue robe with a mandarin collar. I don't know if it was the expression on her face, but her resemblance to her mother was uncanny. I pulled Grandma's picture off the shelf to show it to our friends. Mom seemed to enjoy this visit, but as soon as they left, she drifted off to sleep again.

Soon afterward Mom told me that seeing people was becoming difficult. Some friends still came but it was more purposeful. Friends brought food or sat with Mom so I could take a brief respite. One well-intending friend arranged to have a beautician come to our house because Mom had shared that she was frustrated with her hair. When I gave Mom that news, it set off a firestorm. I saw energy from her that I thought I would never see again. She began by ranting about her privacy and that she felt people were being intrusive. She got out of her chair and stormed into the kitchen. She was swinging her arms, moving about, ranting and raving. The anger tide turned onto me. I had been trying to figure out whether I should take my parents' cats with me or find them another home. I did not know if these cats could adapt to my dogs. Mom clearly wanted me to take the cats. She was angry about one thing, and then she would jump onto something else. I had never seen Mom rage until this moment.

Finally, I said, "Mom, aren't you just upset about what's happening?"

It was like I blew out a candle.

Mom slumped and quietly said, "Yes." We sat down at the kitchen table. I got up to make her some tea. When the tea was ready, I gave it to Mom and sat down with her. Mom was clearly tired again. She said softly, "Melissa, if you only knew what I know." She had said this to me off and on throughout the years, but I never pushed her for the information.

I said, "Mom, if you want to tell me, you had probably better do it. You may not have another chance."

She looked at me intensely and said, "Your dad was gay." Her face was set hard as she said this.

I asked, "How do you know?"

"The doctor told me, during the time of your dad's breakdown," she answered.

I thought, *Boy, did that doctor break confidentiality.* I did not express this to Mom. I knew exactly the timeframe she was talking about.

I said, "Did you ever talk to Dad about it?"

Her face was angry and she said, "No, but your brother suspected it. He told me."

I said, "You know Dad used to play games with the doctors when he was on the psych unit. I remember after he came back home, he was kind of bragging about it. So how can we know for sure if it's true?" I can't say this news completely surprised me. I had questioned Dad's sexual orientation myself, but I had put these thoughts on the back burner.

Mom sat back in her chair and said, "That's true." She then looked at me. "Would you call and apologize for my reaction about the hairdresser?"

I looked at Mom and said, "It's already done."

She sighed with relief. Mom pushed the tea away.

"This doesn't taste right." She slumped a little more and whispered, "I wanted to leave him. I just didn't have the nerve."

I helped Mom back to her chair. Every last ounce of energy was drained from her. I was consumed with sadness. I was sad that Mom had never had the marriage she wanted. She never felt valued in a way she wanted to be by her husband, and Dad wasn't there to say whether he was or wasn't gay. It did not matter now. Mom believed it was true. She had held onto that secret as if it had power. It did have power: the power Mom gave it. It was the sharp pain Mom felt when she was hurt or rejected by Dad. It was the separation it created when she would look at Dad and think, *I know your secret.* I felt so sad for her. I felt sad for Dad too. When he wrote me the note about being concerned about my immortal soul, he might have been concerned about his own soul as well. I was glad that he had come to peace about this before he died. Yet, he had spent his life unfulfilled, living a life that limited his ability to be himself, always in fear and self-reproach. I also felt sad that Matthew and I were denied a close family, partly due to this secret. Yet, for me I knew the resolution I hoped for—that Mom might accept me as I am—was not going to happen in our lifetime. She had been too wounded and angry for too long to accept that what drove a wedge between her and Dad was also a part of me.

# CHAPTER 17

# Pulling Weeds

Sometimes while Mom rested inside, I would walk outside around the yard. Sounds of the neighborhood buzzed along as usual. The hot summer air held smells of an approaching new season. It felt peaceful as life moved aimlessly without any particular direction. I thought about pulling weeds. I read that if we paid attention, we could feel a weed release itself from the earth. I knelt down and began pulling weeds. To my amazement, I could actually feel the weed's roots unravel from the earth. I had to be calm and present for this to happen. If I became impatient, the weed would resist as it clung to the soil and it would tear instead of release. This is not unlike us. Don't we cling to the familiar when we are pulled in another direction? Yet, once we surrender, the transition becomes easier. Was I ready to let go? Was Mom ready to release?

Now the hum of the oxygen concentrator vibrated the walls of the house, breaking an uneasy quietness—a quietness of what's next. I was extremely tired. Mom wanted me to sleep on the couch, but I could not sleep there. I would grab a couple hours of sleep in my bedroom. I never dared fall asleep too deeply for fear of not hearing Mom if she needed me. I had contemplated hiring private help, but things were happening so quickly that there simply wasn't time. No time with long days—it didn't make sense. However, I was becoming concerned. Mom was having more difficulty moving. I knew I could not lift her on my own. The prospect of hiring additional help was definitely becoming a reality.

I had so many plans, but I knew better. Plans usually don't happen as planned. I thought my knowledge of home care would have proven to be more helpful. Instead, I felt helpless. I knew what to do to help Mom, and I was doing it. Mom was receptive to my help, but I always felt I was not helping enough.

I was in the kitchen when I heard Mom call my name. When I entered the living room, she was sitting on the edge of her chair. She could barely speak.

"I can't get air in or out," she whispered in obvious distress.

At that moment I knew she needed more help than I could offer. The oxygen concentrator at home wasn't enough. She was deteriorating by the hour. She was weak and distressed. I asked Mom if she wanted to go to the hospice house. She wanted to go.

I called the hospice nurse. My heart was beating fast. I was anxious about her deteriorating condition. An ambulance was called. Mom wanted to be washed before they arrived.

"It really does come full circle," she said as I bathed her. She looked at me. "What have I done with my life?" She took another breath. "I have done nothing," she whispered.

Emotions overwhelmed me. I knew she was aware the end was near. She had plans and dreams that would never be fulfilled. She was self-evaluating with no time left, and she was too sick to do anything about it.

I said, "Mom, you are who you are. That alone is special. Look at you and the friends you've made in such a short period of time. People really like you. That is a gift unto itself." I didn't say this just to make her feel better. I believed it.

"I suppose that's true," Mom whispered. I could tell she was becoming exhausted.

The hospice nurse told me that the hospice house was full. The ambulance was going to take Mom to a wing at the hospital that was associated with that hospice house. Mom and I continued to wait for the ambulance. Chessie, one of my parents' four cats, was perched on the back of another chair near Mom. She was intensely looking at Mom. Augie, one of Chessie's kittens, who now weighed about twenty pounds, jumped onto Mom's lap. He was her comfort and had been since he was a kitten. Every morning Mom would sit in her chair and she would put a blanket on her arm. Augie would jump onto her lap, lay down, and kneed the blanket as they both drifted off to sleep. Mom was fading as she weakly reached up to pet him. My chest tightened. I knew this probably would be Augie's last time with Mom.

Finally, the ambulance arrived. Augie jumped down. Chessie stayed perched on the chair in a protective stance. She did not run when the EMTs came into the house. She did not run when they put Mom on the gurney. She jumped down as they were ready to take Mom out. This was unusual for Chessie. I wondered how much she understood.

The hospital with the hospice wing was the same hospital Matthew was taken to two days before he committed suicide. It was the same hospital Dad admitted himself to after he threatened to kill himself with tranquilizers and vodka, and it was the same hospital Dad was taken to after Matthew's funeral. Now this hospital held its place for Mom. She seemed to relax when she arrived. I asked the nurse if they would give Mom a bath and wash her hair. They assured me they would do so. Mom didn't say it directly, but I sensed that she wanted me to stay. However, the accommodations weren't exactly comfortable. As it would be, this hospice wing was under renovations. The room only had one straight-backed vinyl chair. It didn't recline. There was another hospital bed in the room. Perhaps it was reserved for another admission. I was extremely tired. Relief washed over me knowing that others were involved in her care. Relief only made me feel more tired. I decided to go back to the house. I hugged Mom and told her I loved her and that I would see her in the morning. She was not very responsive.

When I returned to the house, I called for reinforcements from Vermont. Things had reached the point where I needed help. Annette, my partner, arranged to drive to Vermont the next day.

The highways in Columbus, Ohio, scare me. Actually, any of the big city highways scare me. Perhaps I have become accustomed to the lesser traffic of Vermont. Yet, even people who live in Columbus sometimes get lost on these highways. Mom's friend, again, graciously volunteered to drive me to the hospital in the morning. We missed the exit. It took quite a while to get back on track. It was almost noon when we arrived. When we walked into the room, Mom spread her arms and hugged me. I could tell she was glad to see me. She didn't look any different from the night before. I said, "Mom, what have they done for you?"

She spread her arms again, and whispered, "Nothing."

I was annoyed. I approached the nurses' station. I asked them why Mom had not been bathed or had her hair washed as I had requested last night. They never really answered this question but told me someone would be right in. I went back into Mom's room and sat in the chair beside her bed.

When I told Mom that Annette was coming from Vermont, she slapped her forehead with her hand. It was clear to me that Mom's ability to speak was diminishing. I told Mom earlier that I would only call Annette if things took a turn for the worse. I know she wasn't ready to give up hope. This news frustrated her. Perhaps she thought I had given up hope.

I sat beside Mom for another two hours. No one came to help her. I went back to the nurses' station again. I was frustrated. I was pushing for Mom. She could not push for herself now. Shortly afterward, two care providers came into the room. I left the room to wait in the hallway. I took this opportunity to call Vermont and check on my business and my home. I saw one aide leave the room and return holding a bedpan. A few minutes later they both emerged. Upon returning to the room I found mom rolling back and forth saying, "Too fast, too fast."

I said, "Mom, it's me. They're all done." She settled down. Mom's gown had been changed. I could see that her hair was washed. The care providers were not in her room very long. If anyone could recognize that she was not being cared for conscientiously, it was Mom, even in her deteriorated state. I lifted the sheet to make sure the bedpan was gone. I did not see one, so I sat down again. I was irritated. Mom had been rushed through her care. My mind shot back to working at the nursing home. I knew these care providers were under pressure. I was disappointed in myself. I should have stayed in the room while they bathed her. Mom began moving around in the bed. I thought she might want to roll over. I lifted the sheet and rolled Mom onto her side. Low and behold, there was the bedpan underneath mom! A deep ring was imprinted on her bottom. The bedpan was pushed down into the mattress. That is why I did not see it when I looked. I grabbed the bedpan and flung it across the room as I said a few expletives. The bedpan was empty. No one else was in the room, but knowing Mom, she was glad I was angry.

I stormed to the nurses' station. I was shaking. Having been in their position, I am sure they dreaded seeing me storm down the hallway. They were very apologetic with the exception of one individual who debated the amount of time the bedpan was under Mom. The exact time to me was irrelevant. The ring on her bottom told the whole story. They reassured me that they would speak to the care providers. To me this was of little consequence. I knew it wasn't completely their fault. Again, there was probably too little staff for too many people. We have a health care system that treats masses not individuals. Until we resolve these issues, neglect will continue to happen.

I was trying to protect Mom but not doing very well. I sat beside her again. Mom kicked the sheets and shot me a look to let me know she was frustrated. I did not like being this angry. An overburdened health care system was letting Mom down. I did not like making a scene, but I had my mother to protect.

Shortly after this episode a nurse came into the room. She told us that a room had opened up at the hospice house. Mom would be moved shortly. I called another one of Mom's friends to give me a ride to the hospice house so I could help her settle in for the night. When I told Mom he was coming to give me a ride to the hospice house and then home, she slapped her forehead again.

The hospice house was very calm. By the time I left to meet Annette at the house, I was confident Mom would receive good care. A few hours later, a very tired Annette arrived. She had driven straight from Vermont. Relief washed over me. Now I had a companion for the remainder of this journey.

# CHAPTER 18

# Hesitant Surrender

Annette and I were two Vermonters attempting to survive the insane interstates of Columbus. We almost got nailed in the morning rush traffic on the way to the hospice house. We arrived grateful to be alive. I could immediately see that Mom was well cared for and comfortable when we entered her room. She was asleep. Her face was relaxed. Immediately a nurse came in to update us on her condition.

I woke Mom so she would know I was there. I told her that I planned to stay. She smiled. I knew she had lost her ability to speak. Annette leaned over me and said, "Hi." Mom raised her eyebrows. I intuitively knew what she meant. It was her way of saying, "Look at me now," perhaps followed by one of her favorite sayings, "What will be, will be." I also knew this was a look of acceptance of the moment.

Mom slept most of the time. The nurses checked on her frequently. However, for me there was no real reprieve. I was informed that her being in this facility was only a temporary arrangement. Most likely she would have to return home. I decided not to be overwhelmed by this information. I would take the day as it came. Some of Mom's friends came to visit. However, she could not visit now. So we carried on conversations while sitting around her. In the afternoon a doctor came in to examine Mom. He asked me to go into the hallway with him and told me that she had fluid in her lungs. He asked if I wanted her to go on an antibiotic. This frustrated me. Mom wanted to continue on antibiotics after her emergency room prescription ran out, but when I called her oncologist, he would not order an antibiotic. Now I felt like it was too late. Mom's condition had deteriorated too much. What benefit would the antibiotics give her now? Would she want to be on an antibiotic now? I was very torn with this decision. I did not want to extend Mom's life if she had no quality. The doctor told me that the antibiotic may be disruptive to her intestines. I felt that Mom had enough going on without introducing more disruptions. Did the benefit outweigh the negatives of this medication? I told the doctor, "No, for now," since Mom's condition was deteriorating so rapidly. At this point I wished I had someone else in my life that could help with these decisions. I knew Mom didn't want to die. If I had been told that the antibiotic would bring her back to a point where she could live with quality, I would have said yes in a heartbeat.

I wished Mom would wake up and tell me what she wanted to do. Mom could not wake up. I guess that was my answer. Another doctor, the same doctor who had cared for her on the hospice wing at the hospital, came in to see Mom about an hour later. After examining her, he asked me to go into the hallway. About this time Mom's friends decided to leave.

The doctor said, "I see too much change since yesterday." I felt a sense of relief. Finally someone was seeing what I had been witnessing for the last nineteen days.

I asked, "Do you think she is actively dying now?"

He answered the affirmative and he left to notify the nursing staff. I went back into the room and sat beside Mom. She was receiving six liters of oxygen through a nasal cannula. It was literally a breeze in her face. The doctor explained that the oxygen might make her dying process more difficult. What did I want to do? I certainly did not want her to suffer anymore, but I knew Mom wanted to live. If I stopped the oxygen suddenly, it might be a stressor. I did not want her last memory of me to be one of cutting off her air supply, which she might see as her life source. I asked the nurse to reduce the oxygen but not shut it off.

I sensed that Mom wanted to be alone. Once everyone left the room, including the nurse, I said to her, "Mom, it's just you and me now."

Each breath became shallower than the one before it. Despite the increased dose of morphine and Ativan, Mom was alert. She was struggling to breathe. I could also see her concentration on each breath. Despite her best effort, she was fighting a losing battle.

"You are getting close," I said softly.

Her face became set with determination. Though she could not speak, her expression said everything. I wished I had not said anything. Slowly she began to relax. Suddenly she jerked awake and began vigorously shaking her head back and forth. I do not know why, but I knew she was on her way. I jumped up and held her head with one hand, while I gently stroked the back of her neck with the other hand. I leaned over her.

I softly said, "Let go, Mom," over and over again. She stopped breathing. I began to cry. She started to breathe again. She looked at me. I said, "Mom, let go. I will be okay."

So Mom let go.

I sat beside her bed quietly crying for I don't know how long. I looked at her body in the bed as I felt her presence fill the room. The oxygen was still blowing into her lifeless nostrils. I took a deep breath, reached up, and turned off the oxygen. I got up and left the room to tell the nurse that Mom had died.

I imagined Mom stepping out of her body. Perhaps Dad was helping her. She probably looked at him, giggled in a way that only she could, and said, "Bob, I didn't want to see you so soon." Her gaze would drift beyond Dad to where Matthew and Grandma waited. In an instant she would be filled with such love. It was so enormous that she no longer yearned for the earthly realm. This is my hope for the woman named Charlotte, who was my mom.

# PART 7

# Aging Well

# CHAPTER 19

# Thoughts of Mom

There were times during Mom's illness when she looked so vulnerable. She looked like a little girl sitting in the hospital bed. All I wanted to do was to pick her up, bring her home, and make her better. I felt like my world was falling apart, but I tried not to show it. I felt afraid, overwhelmed, and alone, but I tried not to show it. I missed Mom before she was gone. I longed for the times at home when I would come downstairs in the morning to find Mom sitting in her robe at the kitchen table, reading the newspaper while drinking her decaf. I would smell coffee brewing. She had heard me stirring upstairs and turned the coffee on. I would toast an English muffin that she had specifically gotten for me, knowing I liked them. I would ask her if she wanted a cup of the regular coffee. She would smile and then say, "I'll just have one cup." I would fill her cup and then bring mine to the table. I would butter my toasted English muffin and sit down with Mom. She would share some of the news. We would talk about my life in Vermont, people we both knew, and of course, Dad. Our conversations could drift anywhere comfortably. Before I knew it, the coffee pot was empty, and it was time to get on with the day. It's funny how these simple times are such treasures to me now. Oh, how I miss those moments. Oh, how I miss Mom's voice and her smile. I hope I showed her how much I loved her.

It was so difficult, but I tried not to show her how much I was feeling as she was going through the dying process. Perhaps I should have been more open with her. I just don't know. In fact I didn't even want to acknowledge to myself the extent of my grief. In the end when I told her to let go, it was only because there seemed to be no other direction. She had wanted us to take a train ride across the country. She had wanted to be healthy enough to dance. Mom loved to dance. She had told me that she and Dad danced only once. She could almost feel him counting. It bothered her. When Mom danced, she felt the music. She moved freely and joyfully. Perhaps my parents' one dance told their story in a way. Yet, I know she loved him. Once I asked her why she didn't date

Dick instead. She said, "I didn't feel that way about Dick." She said that her feelings were strong for Dad. I only wish that in their later years my parents had talked more. So much pain might have been alleviated. Sometimes I feel there was so much more to say to Mom. Yet, when I think about it, we talked a lot. We amended a lot. I just miss her presence and our connection. I know on some level that our connection remains. When I think of Mom, I think of softness and fun, intertwined with sophistication.

A few months after Dad died, Mom purchased a knockout rose bush. She planted it beside the corner of the front doorway landing. Apparently she must have expressed to a friend that she liked this particular rose bush, as that friend showed up at the house with another knockout rose. Mom planted that bush at the base of the landing near the driveway. Both bushes had white blossoms. Mom's last summer was hot and dry. Her roses didn't wither, but they didn't thrive either. On the morning of Mom's funeral, I went out onto the landing to retrieve the newspaper, and there was Mom's rose bush in full bloom. The bush near the driveway had not changed. The one Mom had picked out and planted was bursting with bloom on a hot summer morning which had seen no rain. I smiled at the beauty of her message, and I knew that she was with me on that very difficult day.

CHAPTER 20

# Thoughts of Dad

When I was about three years old, Dad would come into my bedroom and scoop me out of bed in the wee hours of the morning. He would take me into the kitchen to make me a cup of tea with honey. He would serve it to me in a Bennington pottery mug, just like the one he used. So there we were, me and Dad, sitting at the kitchen table at two in the morning. Dad would make conversation with me, but I don't remember what we talked about. I just knew I liked it. The following mornings I would brag to Matthew that I had tea with Dad. Matthew wanted to do it too, so one night Dad brought Matthew out into the kitchen as well. He put him in the highchair and gave him some tea. Matthew just drooped in the chair and fell asleep.

Dad, was a complex man—a man I didn't know in many respects. Yet, many who knew him have told me that I have many of his characteristics. He was a man who as a child was abandoned by those closest to him, with the exception of his grandmother. Dad wore a shield; he only exposed what he wanted people to see. Of course the shield would get heavy, and we, as his family, got glimpses of the man behind it. He may have been a man who lived one life while yearning for another. He buried so many emotions. Sometimes these buried feelings would explode leaving a lot of debris. His past haunted him. He had a father who rejected him and a mother who gave him up and could not provide a stable foundation when she had to take him after her mother died. This unfinished, unhealed past all came crashing down on Mom, Matthew, and me. After Matthew died, his explosions stopped. He didn't talk about making this change, at least not to me. He simply, or not so simply, changed how he behaved toward everyone.

Dad bore the weight of Matthew's death the rest of his life. Each Christmas he would cut off a sliver from the trunk of the Christmas tree. On this sliver he would write a message to Matthew and then place it in a basket on a shelf in Matthew's bedroom. This bedroom remained unchanged until Dad died.

As for me, each time I visited home after our reconnection, I would find fresh flowers and a card on my bedroom bureau. The card welcomed me home. I didn't realize until he was gone that Dad was the motivator behind this welcome. After he died, it stopped.

Dad was passionate about so many things. He cared about people. He believed in peace. He believed in equality. Mom believed in these things too. Perhaps that was part of their bond. As he laid in the reclining chair at home in the living room, close to death, the priest from their church came to the house to give him the sacrament for the sick.

After he finished, the priest said to Dad, "Just think, Bob—you will be able to listen to the real Frank Sinatra any time you want." He said this knowing how much Dad loved that generation of music.

Dad whispered as best he could to the priest, "I was kind of hoping for something a little more glorious."

Well, Dad, here's to something more glorious.

# CHAPTER 21

# No Reprieve

A warm breeze interrupted my inner silence. I stood near Mom's gravesite. We had talked about it. She was concerned about my being alone after she died. I kind of brushed it off saying, "I'll be okay." Now, I wasn't so sure. My entire immediate family was in this graveyard. I was no longer a sister or daughter to anyone living. Yet, for now all I desired was quiet and peace. I let the warm sun-drenched summer breeze consume me. It complemented my numbness. How many times I stood in this place with my parents, and then with just Mom, and now only me. I suddenly felt very alone.

The world we have created does not allow for escape or reprieve. We have made things so complicated. Now I had the daunting task of wrapping things up in Ohio. After Mom's services were over, I returned to a house that once felt like home. With Annette's help we went room to room, gradually taking it apart and sorting it out. Matthew's room was the most difficult for me. My parents had given away most of his clothes over the years. They filled any open spaces in the drawers with all of my brother's life, from his birth certificate to gas receipts from the seventies.

Mom had prepared for her death. That made this part of my journey a little easier. She wanted an auctioneer to come to the house. So that is what I did. After that was done, I gave some things to the neighbors. I gave some things to charity. Some things I wanted the remaining family to have, while other things I could not give away. Their value only held memories for me, so I had to put them out in front of the house for the garbage company to pick up. I was glad to see that some of these items had been taken up before the garbage came. I was grateful when a young man next door was thrilled with Dad's book collection. Dad would have appreciated his enthusiasm. I encouraged him to take any book he desired. Some of my parents' friends helped me clean up and paint the house. The last two days went like clockwork. When I had a need, it seemed as if someone appeared out of nowhere to meet that need. Before I knew it, the house was ready to put on the market and a realtor placed a sale sign on the front lawn.

All of my past was now in an eight-by-eight trailer hitched onto the back of my car. My parents' four cats were in carriers on the backseat. Annette waited in the car as I walked room to room in this house which was my home for so many years. This house held the complexities of each of us. It held great sadness. It also held healing and love. For me it was time to say good-bye. I stood in my bedroom, which still had furniture. I had arranged for Mom's housekeeper to take it in trade for watching over the house while it was on the market. It struck me: the only room that was full was mine, and I was the only one of this family remaining on this earth. I went outside and walked around the yard. I looked at the trees and plants Dad had planted. I stood on the patio where we as a family had spent so much time. I remembered the good times. I took a deep breath. I breathed in all that used to be in this home, be it comfort, sadness, or hope. I wished for happiness for whoever would eventually occupy this space that held so many memories for me. I returned to the car and we drove away for the last time.

Annette and I drove back to Vermont in one day. We were both exhausted—Annette more than I since she drove the entire way. There had been too many changes for me. It did not make sense to me. I had spent almost my entire adult life limiting my time with my parents, and now I missed them so much. Perhaps it was because we had made amends and our relationship was healed. I am so grateful for the relationship we developed. We weren't perfect and some things remained unresolved; yet, the foundation of love remained intact and strong.

Now I had my life to figure out. Everything felt different to me. I could not get my heart back into the business. I just went through the motions. I had no energy. The staff primarily kept the business going. I didn't feel good about my apathy, but I didn't know how to change it.

On the one year anniversary of Mom's death, which also happened to be Grandma's birthday, my cat Lucky was attacked by a dog. His injuries were so extensive that I had to let him go. Two days later, muddy water came roaring down our street as the creek near the house could no longer handle Hurricane Irene's rain. It was pure chaos. We thought we had prepared, but none of us really anticipated a flash flood of this capacity. We got as many animals out of the house as possible before the water got too high. I stood on the hill in back of the house and watched the water surround the neighborhood. I watched our wood pile float away. I watched the rapids race down the street. I felt so powerless. All Annette and I could do was pray that the water did not reach the second floor where the rest of the animals remained. We lucked out. The water receded before it reached the second floor.

A friend opened her home to us, even to our cats and rabbits. A coworker of Annette's let us keep the dogs at his home. Never had I seen so much mud. It surrounded the house. It surrounded the neighborhood. In some homes, it filled their basements. I usually ran the business from the downstairs of my home. I had to move the office upstairs into our living space until the downstairs was rebuilt and inhabitable again. Our damage was minimal compared to others. At least we had a home. There were many who lost everything. I didn't allow for feeling sorry for myself. There was so much to do. Friends and strangers offered to help, but I didn't know what to tell them to do. It all seemed so overwhelming. I had to keep the business going. There were people in need, and that need did not cease because of the flood. I knew at this point that I needed to make a change in my life. I was afraid of change. Yet, life has its way of letting you know it's going to happen, fear or no fear.

Burnout is insidious. I have always said a good care provider knows when it's time to take a break. Even before Dad died I knew I needed to change what I was doing. I was burning out. I made a promise to myself years before that I would not allow myself to stagnate. Now the time had come for me to jump into the unknown. But these changes did not come quickly or easily. I had people dependent on the business for care and employees who needed jobs. So I changed my environment. I moved to a new home, which would hopefully prove to be safer in the event of another natural disaster.

This geographical change offered little relief for my burnout. During the fifteen years of running the business, I had had two business partners. The last few years I ran it alone. I lost friends whom I had hired. I gained friends as well. I had also gone through several eye surgeries to improve my vision. Life had been a constant stream of activity. Losing Mom seemed to take my steam. I was tired, life tired. A change was needed, but the direction unknown. It was time to take a risk again. It was a difficult decision, but I sold the business. I essentially eliminated much that was familiar to me in Vermont, but I felt so strongly that this is what I needed to do. I needed to take time.

# CHAPTER 22

# Myself, Aging, and Margaret

I looked in the mirror. Who was that woman looking back at me? My gray roots were showing and I felt tired. I looked like Grandma. I was not ready for this. I rushed to color my hair. For so many years I wanted to protect the elderly, but I wasn't ready to be elderly yet. But I thought, *why not?* Well, my entire life, like everyone else who is exposed to the media, I was taught that aging is bad. Avoid it at all costs. If you have wrinkles, cover them. If you have sagging skin, tighten it. A person who ages well is supposed to look young and act young—the main message being, "It is good to be young and bad to be old." So there I was at fifty-six years old, looking in the mirror at a middle-aged woman. I could deal with the wrinkles, but I didn't like the sagging skin.

Should I hate who I am because I am aging? I find myself being a targeted consumer for insurances, medical alert systems, and medications. I am also eligible for senior discounts. Perhaps I should consider taking more medication, as it is presented that older people should take lots of medicine. However, the people I knew who aged well were on as little medication as possible. They also had wrinkles, sagging skin, and bodies that didn't work so well sometimes. Yet, they had something about themselves that made people smile. They had joy, insight, grace, and a sense of humor. They did not mind who they were and accepted their conditions but did not surrender to them. To me, that is aging well.

Aging isn't easy. I would challenge any triathlete to live in a ninety-five-year-old body. Aging is unique to each individual soul that occupies a body. It is as if our body is the sculpture and our life the sculpting tool. Why do we dread the inevitable? It would seem to me more beneficial to embrace the changes of age and value their lessons.

Now I resolve to look in the mirror, see myself as I am today, and like who I see. I will appreciate my existence in the here and now as I am. My time will come to die. Therefore, I must choose to live well. I will move my body so I can keep moving. I will use my mind so I can keep thinking. I will reach out to friends so I won't be lonely. I will give when I can, as that makes me grateful. If I become burdened with illness or disease, I will do my best to cope well and be grateful for any help I receive. And I will be creative, as that connects me to all.

My thoughts often drift back to the nursing home and my unrest that even after thirty-four years not much has been done to improve the loneliness and rejection people feel in facilities. I remember Margaret. Just because she couldn't walk, couldn't talk, couldn't eat by herself, it was assumed that she wouldn't know that her husband had died. So no one told her. Perhaps they thought she wouldn't notice. I saw her eyes as she watched him walk down the hallway. She couldn't express it, but she was glad to see him. I saw it in her eyes, and I know her husband saw it too. I don't know if she could have measured the days, but without him coming, without that loving person being there every day, I am sure her days seemed long. She couldn't even express that she missed him. Perhaps it was the emptiness in her stare or her tight lips that refused to allow a spoonful of food to enter her mouth that said it all. Perhaps this is how she cried. Shortly after his death her condition began to decline. She was in bed more than the chair. One of the nurses called some of the remaining family. They said, "Let us know when she dies." The nurse was infuriated.

No one came to visit Margaret. But she would not die. She lay in that bed, her skin yellow; even the whites of her eyes were bloodshot and yellow. She could not move. She could not eat. She could only breathe. She lay like this for over two weeks. It bothered us to watch her suffer. One evening after my shift ended, I felt strongly compelled to go into Margaret's room before I left for the night. She was lying on her back, breathing loudly with her eyes wide open, as if she was terrified. I leaned over her and spoke directly into her ear so she could hear me over her own loud breathing.

I said gently but directly, "Margaret, we love you. I love you. It is okay."

Having said that, I softly touched her hand and left her room feeling extremely sad. A few hours later Margaret died. I felt then, and still feel today, that Margaret was waiting for someone to care enough to say good-bye.

# Conclusion

There are still too many Margarets. These people are in facilities, in their homes, and on the street. Perhaps it is you. Perhaps it is someone you love or care about. These people all have something in common: they need help and feel alone. Yet, they may not even acknowledge this to themselves. They may feel trapped in a place, in their life, or in their own body. These people may feel like they don't fit in, and all too often, they are treated like an outcast. Therefore, they/we give up. They give up on themselves and we give up on them.

As depressing as this sounds, there is always hope. Not everyone takes this journey. Also, anyone's journey can be redirected. The problems which elderly and vulnerable people face every day are too vast for any one individual to solve. Perhaps the solution lies within each one of us.

When I started this book, I thought I was going to write a book only about the elderly. As I proceeded with my writing, I realized this book was about all humanity. Our elderly can offer us so much by who they are today—be it that they lived well or lived unwell, be it that they grew and blossomed with age or they became stuck and rigid. Each person offers us the entirety of their life. Listen to their wisdom, or lack of it. See their aged bodies of grace, or bodies riddled with disease. Observe their inner peace, or fear. We cannot ignore their lessons, for they guide us in our life choices. Someday, if we live long enough, we will be that aged person offering our life experiences to all humanity.

The next time you see a person of age, realize that they have grown into it, as you may someday. I like it when an older person says, "I have earned each line on my face," and they say it with pride. Instead of ridiculing or fearing the lines of age, I hope we learn to embrace them. For they are the roadmap of each of our lives, be it sorrow or laughter that drove each line deeper. It is unique to each of us and sets us apart by our own characteristics.

After all, who are these vulnerable people who cannot walk, talk, bathe themselves, eat without help, or even think? Who is the baby born who will never grow up to be whole and active? Who are the homeless, alcoholics, drug addicts, criminals, and conformists? Who are the politicians, religious leaders, and executives? Who are the artists, entertainers, and dreamers? They are all of us in different sizes, shapes, abilities, and ideologies. Each feels sadness and joy, has loved and has lost, has cried and has laughed, has felt cared for or neglected, and has felt acknowledged or forgotten.

When the time comes for each of us to leave this earth, it does not matter our status in life, for we are all equal and leave as we arrived: naked and vulnerable. Therefore, value yourself enough to make changes and live well. When you see vulnerability in another, do not divert your eyes. Allow yourself to recognize that their vulnerabilities, as well as your own, are part of humanity's greatest strength. The lessons of the elderly and vulnerable people, though perhaps invisible, are priceless. Embrace these qualities in yourself, and if true empathy calls on you to reach out, do it! Allow the wounds of the broken to heal, and let us build deeper connections which will bring us to a new level of being human.

# About the Author

Melissa Forgey has worked and advocated for the elderly for thirty-two years, fifteen of those years as the owner of a home health business. She has a BA in fine arts and uncompleted nurses' training due to her visual impairment. She currently lives on a small farm in Vermont.